Design in Object Technology 2
The Annotated Class of 1994
Backstories and reflections

Series on Object-Oriented Design
Series on **Object-Oriented** **Design**

Alistair Cockburn

"The Germans believe that he is best read while inebriated,
which is why they yell "Proust" before they drink."
https://en.uncyclopedia.co/wiki/Marcel_Proust
Just sayin.

© Alistair Cockburn 2022 all rights reserved
ISBN 978-1-7375197-2-0
Humans and Technology Press
32 W 200 S #504
Salt Lake City, UT 84101
v1.01-220925-1726

Preface to the *Annotated Class of 1994*

In 1991 I was hired by the IBM Consulting Group to create a methodology for their object-technology projects. An early "agile" methodology, its emphasis was on incremental development, requirements in use cases, and design using responsibilities.

We applied the methodology in 1994 on a fixed-price, fixed-scope project that integrated COBOL programs with a sizable Smalltalk application via a relational database. Bid as a $10M, 18-month, 50-person project, it delivered on time at a cost of about $15M. The client was happy with the result and the system was still being maintained ten years later, so it was considered a successful project. The project is written up in detail as "project Winifred" in the 1997 book *Surviving Object-Oriented Projects*.

At the start of the project, I gave a week-long course to the entire team. it covered incremental development, use cases, responsibilities, an early hexagonal architecture, methodologies, whatever they would need to function on the project. The people in the course knew nothing about these concepts at the time.

The first book, *"Class of 1994"*, was no more and no less than slides from that course, all 214 of them. To honor its historical purpose, I made no changes to the slides. What you saw is what I taught back then.

What I have done in this book is again, not to tell the course itself. The slides are fairly self-explanatory. I have written two sorts of comments, addressing these questions:

- What was the backstory behind the ideas then becoming mainstream?
- What do I think of them now? Still valid, passé, superseded?

It is these commentaries, more even than the course content, that may be of interest to practitioners today.

Because this is a commentary on a historical document, I do not attempt to repair any slides or update the course content itself. This is just as I showed it to them. What I have added as fresh content are my recollections from that time and my reflections on what has happened since.

This book may be of interest to those people who were practicing object-oriented design back in the 1990s. They will be interested to see how I presented topics that were current back then, and how I feel about them now. Designers arriving since 2001 may find this discourse interesting, to not only learn what life was like back then, but also to learn some of the historical underpinnings of what the best designers do today.

I hope you enjoy it.

Alistair Cockburn
Gulfport, Sept 2022

> *"...he wrote with a pen in each hand,*
> *And explained all the while in a popular style*
> *Which the Beaver could well understand."*
> -- Lewis Carroll, *The Hunting of the Snark* (Fit the Fifth)

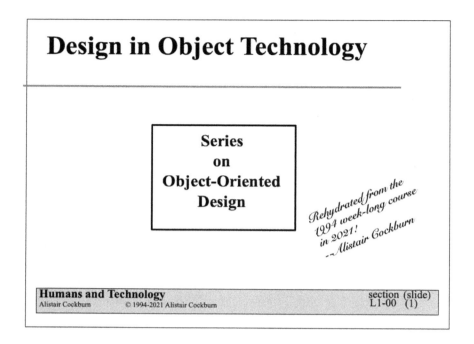

That course title, eh? Bet you didn't even think about it.

In 1992, writing the methodology for the IBM Consulting Group's methodology for OO projects, I had to decide what to do about the then-standard phases in a project: Requirements, Analysis, Design, Code.

The problem was the word "Analysis". For those arriving recently and never having seen these phases, the intent of the "Analysis" phase was to come up with a technology-independent model of the business. That was the standard thinking at the time.

It turns out to be impossible, as I came to discover, and as we generally understand these days. There are always multiple valid models of the business. None is uniquely "correct", strange as that may seem. Parallel and proximate vocabulary allows us to describe the world in many ways, all internally consistent, valid and meaningful. On top of that, the technology being selected affects which one of the multiple valid models makes a good technology-sensitive design for a given project.

I came to understand that in 1992 while designing the methodology for IBM, and then encountered it with a vengeance on real project "Winifred" in 1994-5. I wrote about that experience at some length in my 1997 book *Surviving Object-Oriented Projects*. I also taught it as a core part of my OO design and business modeling courses. It was a hard pull back in the 1990s.

Concluding that "Object-Oriented Analysis" didn't make sense either as a phase or as a business activity, I dropped it from my vocabulary. I am happy to say that the industry eventually caught up with this idea, and we no longer have "Analysis" phases on most software projects.

This wasn't generally known or accepted in 1994, so companies would call me and ask for an "OO Analysis" course.

It took a lot of sales cycles before I worked out that what they really wanted was a sort of OO Design class, but without programming, so their business people could create any of those valid business models and then dialog with the programmers. The programmers would hopefully counter with a different, also valid business model that fit the technology and project characteristics better, and the two groups could iterate back and forth over the models until they found a nice one that both expressed the business well and also implemented well.

This line of thinking was expanded by Eric Evans in his book *Domain Driving Design* and is carried on by the DDD community still.

So in the sales call, I would say, "Well, I don't have an 'analysis' course, because I don't think that activity exists, but I do have a Design in Object Technology course in which I show your business analysts and also the programmers how to create an OO model they can use to talk with other business people and programmers."

And they would say, "Yes, that's what we want."

In this way, I learned that they didn't know or care about "analysis" as a phase, what they really wanted was some conversation to happen and some forward movement.

This I can do.

Being stubborn about the nonsense of the term "analysis" in the context of software design projects, I carefully never called my course "Object-Oriented Analysis & Design" as was common at the time, but called it "Design in Object Technology".

I am delighted to say that no company ever complained about the name of the course, or the contents.

So that's why the course is entitled "Design in Object Technology".

Welcome to slide 1 of 214 :).

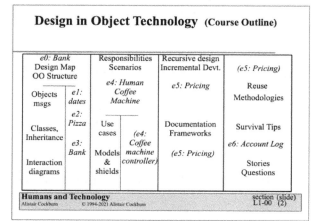

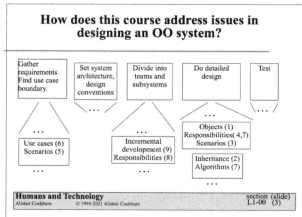

In 1994, it was common for these courses to last a week. Shifting the mind to OO design was really a big story, very difficult, changing a lot of habits.

It was critical at that time to teach people incremental, iterative design and delivery, a strategy that was rarely practiced in the 90s. They also needed to learn writing requirements with the then-new use cases technique instead of numbered requirements or just loose paragraphs. Also needed was enough understanding of why OO code looked so different and what that meant for creating models of the business.

Having to build from nothing, teaching to old-school programmers who probably programmed in BASIC or C, the course starts with why OO programs are different from ordinary programs, and then moves through architecture, requirements gathering with use cases, design using responsibilities, incremental development, and so on.

This particular course was given at the beginning of a large (50 people) project using Smalltalk technology connected to a relational database and COBOL mainframe programs. It was used to introduce all the concepts that the team would need over the next 15 months, synchronize them vocabulary and expected behavior. The project "Winifred" is described in detail in *Surviving Object-Oriented Projects* (an appropriate title at the time!).

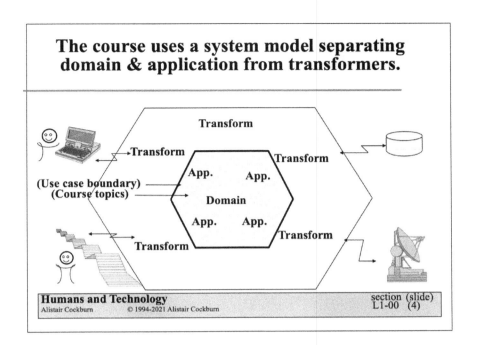

This is the earliest picture of the Hexagonal Architecture I find. It is not totally correct by today's standards, because it shows different technologies connected to the different facets. These days I insist on drawing multiple technologies connected to any one facet, because that is the point of the architecture. You can read all about Hexagonal Architecture at https://alistair.cockburn.us/hexagonal-architecture/ and in the excellent long explanation written by Juan Manuel Garrido de Paz in "Hexagonal Me" at https://jmgarridopaz.github.io/.

Hexagonal Architecture says to separate the application under design from anything in the real world with a pure programming interface, so that the application in essence is just talking to the ether. Then it is indifferent as technologies are changed, whether graphical user interface, or batch jobs, or test cases; or databases, or files as data, or even looping back test cases.

Hexagonal Architecture slowly became clear to me over the next ten years. In 2003, I finally started the long description, which I published on my site in 2005. Some years later the Domain Driven Design (DDD) community adopted it as a core practice, because it keeps the outer-world technology from infiltrating the domain model. Netflix used and wrote about it in 2020: https://netflixtechblog.com/ready-for-changes-with-hexagonal-architecture-b315ec967749.

We did not develop the idea much in the course, mostly I just said something like: "Just put an interface at the boundaries of the application, don't let outside technology in."

As it turned out, on that very project, the people responsible for linking the application to the database didn't do that. It cost the project multiple weeks of delay when they decided to change the database mapping technology. Sad faces all around.

Yeah, use Hexagonal Architecture.

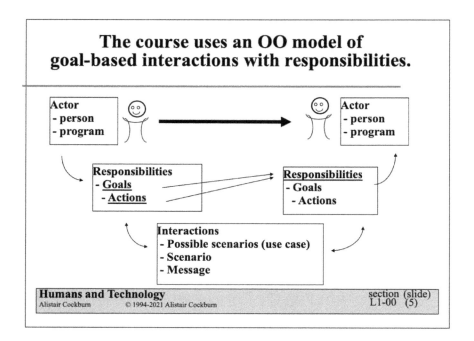

This was one of the most profound images I ever produced. It was the result of thinking about OO design and use cases for several years, and slowly discovering the unity across both.

Interactions are recursive, in the sense that we use a nickname for a lot of specific interactions, as with "I spoke with Kim yesterday". If we open that fat interaction up, we find, "We greeted each other, checked in with each other, discussed our upcoming event, and said good-bye". Each of those would have involved multiple interactions: hugs, handshakes, sentences, head nods, and so on. This notion of interaction as recursive is core. Interactions consist of interactions.

An actor is a person or a program. An actor has responsibilities, such as to complete a project, buy something, answer questions, or do things. To carry out their responsibilities, the actor sets goals and takes an action or initiates an interaction with another actor. That other actor promises things as part of their responsibilities, and so we are now linked to interactions.

Responsibilities are recursive, goals are recursive, actions are recursive, actors can be recursive, and interactions are recursive. (Are you confused, yet? I hope not. Hang on.) This recursiveness is natural in our normal speaking and we don't pay attention when we make use of it in normal dialog. But when we get to writing down requirements and discussing design, we need to be able to move up and down the stack in a controlled way.

Interactions come in sequences, any one of which is a concrete scenario. When we discuss all the things that can go wrong and right in related scenarios, we bundle all those scenarios up into what Ivar Jacobson called "use cases" (more on them later, a whole module's worth).

Yeah, and of course use cases are recursive, also, why not. Confusing when you aren't used to it, but actually natural to human communication and core to keeping the vocabulary under control.

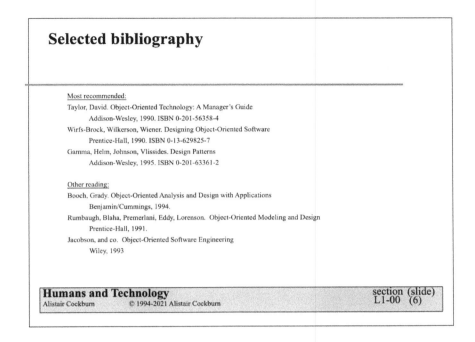

These were the books that were popular in the day.

The David Taylor book was a simple guide to OO programs and their consequences, written as airplane reading for execs. It was actually a pretty good book, sadly out of print by now.

The book *Designing Object-Oriented Software* by Rebecca Wirfs-Brock with Wilkerson and Wiener was and still is foundational. It tightened down all the knowledge about responsibilities as originally created by Ward Cunningham and Kent Beck in the late 1980s. It formed the basis for the methodology I used and taught. Fortunately, Rebecca stayed in the game and produced an updated version in 2002 with Alan McKean: *Object Design: Roles, Responsibilities, and Collaborations*.

The Design Patterns book was and still is the foundational book on OO design patterns.

The other books, by Booch, Rumbaugh, and Jacobson, described methodologies that we wouldn't be using but would be good for people to have in their peripheral vision, if they were interested in reading.

This was/is the end of the preamble to the course.

The next module is a unique lecture, "Object Software's Difference".

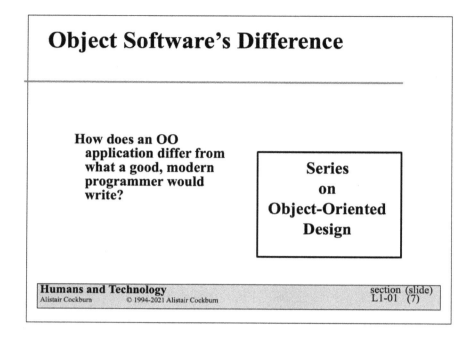

Back in the early 1990s few people knew anything about OO design or programming, and wanted to know what the big deal was.

This was a lecture I gave on almost a monthly basis from 1992 to 1995 to execs, business analysts, even sales people.

Our department's salesman said to me after the talk, "So, if all I remember from this talk is the little blue box at the top, will that be all right?" And I said, "Perfect". :)

These days, almost every programmer uses OO programming to some extent, and don't even think about it, much less why anyone cares in what way it might be different.

For those who know object-oriented programming from the 1990s, you might be surprised at where I went with this lecture. I was looking at what about OO design caused a difference in the methodologies used. See if you can see it coming :)

Most of the slides are self-explanatory, I don't need to speak aloud what each slide shows. Take a look.

The essence of an application is a matrix of functions and data structures.

	□	○	/	AB	✽✾
create	□	□	□	□	□
alter	□	□			□
shift	□	□	□	□	□
volume?	□	□	□		
stats?	□	□	□	□	□

Humans and Technology
Alistair Cockburn   © 1994-2021 Alistair Cockburn

section (slide)
L1-01   (8)

In modular programs, the matrix elements are kept separate, connected by switches at the functions.

	□	○	/	AB	✽✾
create	▣	□	□	□	□
alter	▣	□	□		□
shift	▣	□	□	□	□
volume?	▣	□	□		
stats?	▣	□	□	□	

Humans and Technology
Alistair Cockburn   © 1994-2021 Alistair Cockburn

section (slide)
L1-01   (9)

Yeah, okay, I'll guess maybe you are surprised that two-dimensional shapes are supposed to have volumes. This talk was given in the early 1990s, and I moved so fast no one was paying attention at that level. I was shocked when I opened the old talk and saw *"rectangles : volume?"* What?

It should be "area?" Ah well, I have to present these slides exactly as they were, so we live with it.

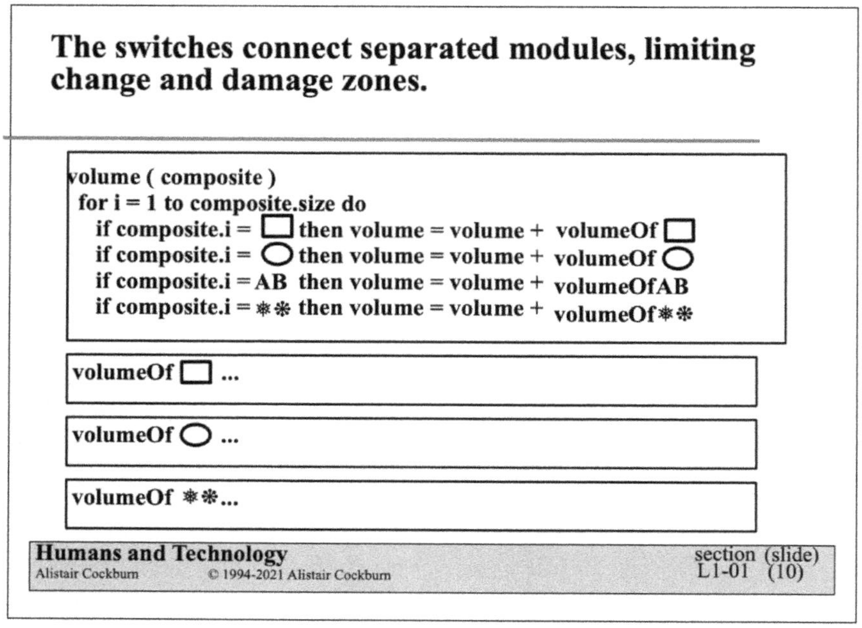

The switches connect separated modules, limiting change and damage zones.

```
volume ( composite )
  for i = 1 to composite.size do
    if composite.i = □ then volume = volume + volumeOf □
    if composite.i = ○ then volume = volume + volumeOf ○
    if composite.i = AB then volume = volume + volumeOfAB
    if composite.i = ✳✳ then volume = volume + volumeOf✳✳
```

volumeOf □ ...

volumeOf ○ ...

volumeOf ✳✳...

Humans and Technology
Alistair Cockburn   © 1994-2021 Alistair Cockburn

section (slide)
L1-01   (10)

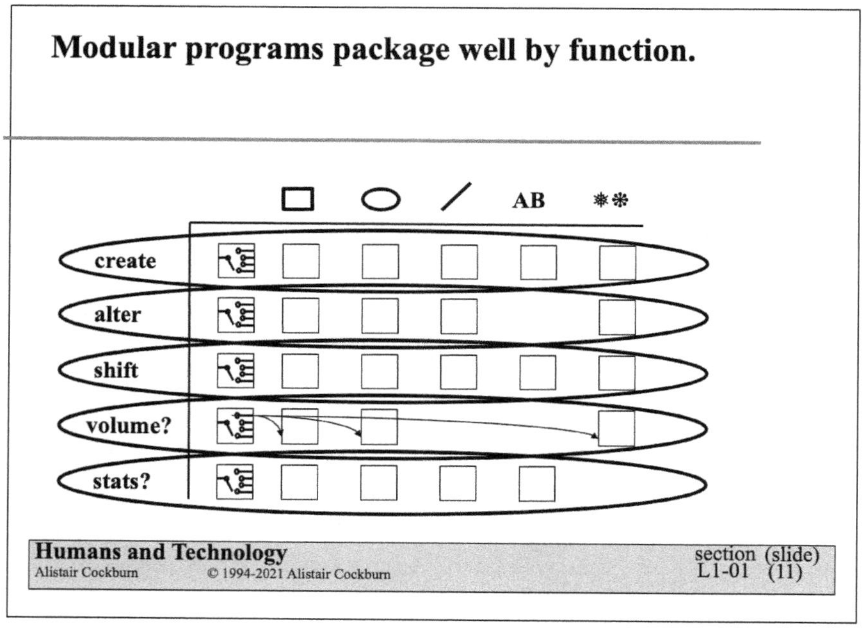

Modular programs package well by function.

	□	○	/	AB	✳✳
create					
alter					
shift					
volume?					
stats?					

Humans and Technology
Alistair Cockburn   © 1994-2021 Alistair Cockburn

section (slide)
L1-01   (11)

There is the essence that I chose: That "normal" programs had procedures that mixed together their data types, and that this causes a certain cost in program maintenance. Watch ...

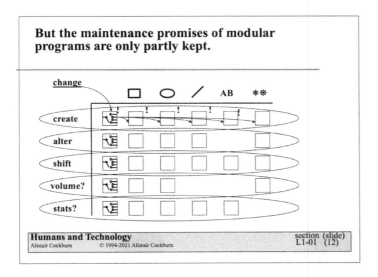

The key voiceover here is that if you touch any line in a file, every line is suspect because of minor typos you didn't notice.

If you touch the create/alter/anything function, then any data connected to that might be compromised, and it will take a lot of work to track down these effects.

For the sharply tuned reader: yes, that's polymorphism right there. I had the misfortune to implement polymorphic switches manually in Prolog in the late 1980s. I lived that cascading damage from typos, daily.

The simple voiceover here is just that a sharp programmer will notice the similarity in all the switching code and put it in one place, a small meta-module that will live outside the application programmer's work.

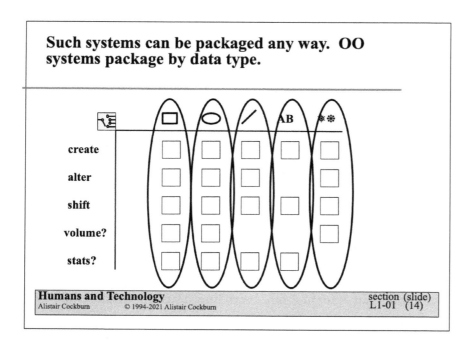

And then the system's programmer puts the switching code into the system itself, away from the application programmers, so all applications get the same benefit.

This is the little blue box our salesman wanted to remember. :)

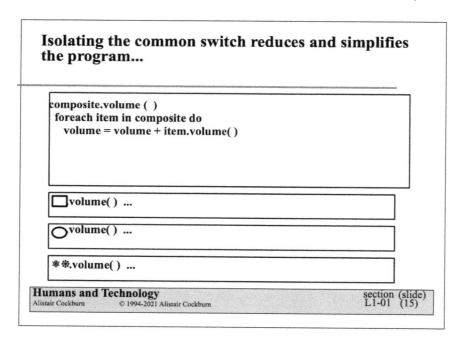

Since the switching code has been put into the operating system, we can no longer make typos in it. All of the functions of all of the data types are separated, so when we blow one up, we are less likely to blow up a bunch of them. So far, it looks really attractive, right?

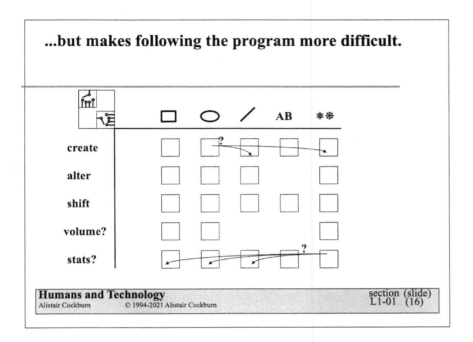

...but makes following the program more difficult.

section (slide)
L1-01   (16)

Not many people in 1994 talked about the downsides of OO programs. Most were missionary zealots who couldn't accept anything negative about their preferred technology.

However, just having a soup of functions and data types with a magic switching module makes code understanding much harder. A later evolution to event-based designs made it even harder. Debugging mistakes in a running system could be a nightmare, since there was no visual connection between parts of the program.

Oh, and that double blue box thing was me turning the switching logic from horizontal to vertical, to match the file modularization by object type. A bit complicated and dramatic, but that was me in 1994: very exact, even when it made things more confusing.

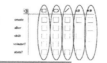

"OO": switching mechanism; less code, unconnected; modularized by object.

1. OO programs require external mechanisms to carry the common switching code.

   ...in C++ it is provided by the compiler.

   ...in Smalltalk it is provided by the run-time.

2. OO programs facilitate modularization by data type (the "objects").

3. OO programs should be shorter, but control flow harder to understand.

Humans and Technology
Alistair Cockburn   © 1994-2021 Alistair Cockburn

section (slide)
L1-01 (17)

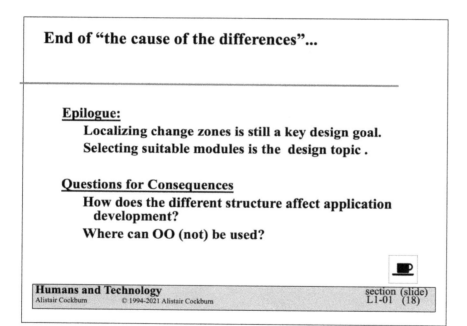

End of "the cause of the differences"...

Epilogue:

Localizing change zones is still a key design goal.

Selecting suitable modules is the design topic .

Questions for Consequences

How does the different structure affect application development?

Where can OO (not) be used?

Humans and Technology
Alistair Cockburn   © 1994-2021 Alistair Cockburn

section (slide)
L1-01 (18)

End of that cute little lecture. How odd to all read that 27 years later :)

(Check out the coffee cup in the corner -- Must be time for a coffee break!)

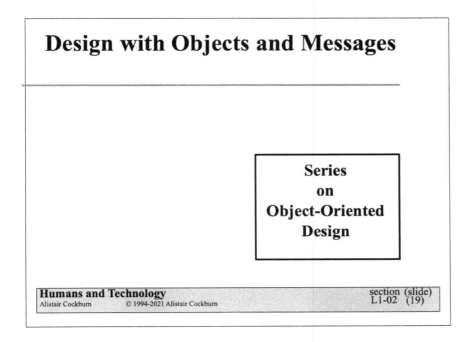

This next module is the first of three modules that introduce objects.

I started with just simple objects: What is an "object"? and, How can we think of them interacting in a way that allows us to design?

Then, moving to classes and inheritance, and how those affect how we design.

With an interlude to explore interaction diagrams and how we can use them.

Finally, introducing "responsibilities" (thanks to Ward Cunningham, Kent Beck and Rebecca Wirfs-Brock) as the central unifying concept that allows us to make good designs.

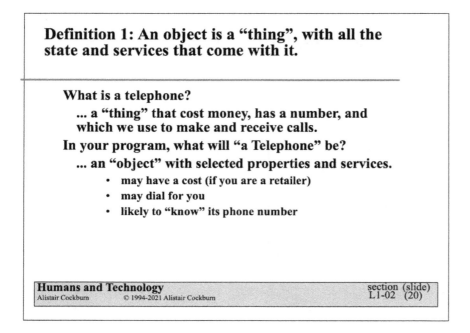

This was the central promise and difference with object-oriented design: that services and data are joined, so that the two rely on and change each other.

It is odd to think of an old-school telephone as offering services, I mean, it just sat there. But inside the software, it can make sense.

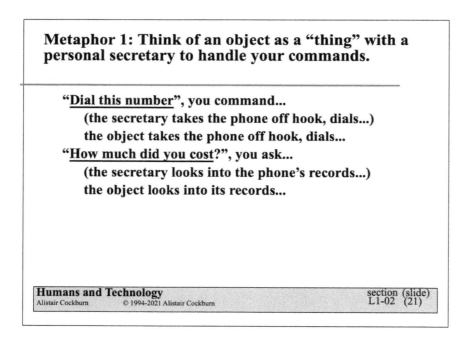

What we are after is to create a *bureaucracy* inside the software, a fake organization of fake "people" pretending to be various inanimate objects, carrying out services on their behalf.

It's weird, but produces some great designs.

Oddly, people are very good at designing bureaucracies. Max Weber, a German scientist, defined *bureaucracy* as a "highly structured, formalized, and also an impersonal organization." (https://www.toppr.com/guides/fundamentals-of-economics-and-management/evolution-of-management-thought/bureaucratic-theory-by-max-weber/).

People are very good at saying, "That's not my job" and "Why are those two people talking to each other?" :) By playing on this ability, even beginner designers can cut up the design into pieces that fit good theoretical models of how software should be designed. (For you experienced and detailed readers, that is coupling and cohesion as the theory, with reduced trajectory of change for the targeted benefit.)

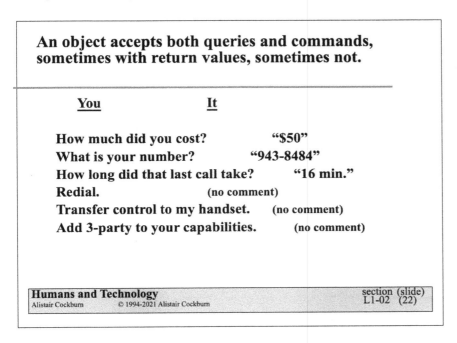

Recall, this was in 1994, and smart phones weren't invented yet, so it was really weird to think of asking one of those old black phones to know how much it cost. I mean, what? (Yes, really, that's what I used to think whenever I saw this slide.)

However, if you shift to thinking of a bureaucracy, where the phone was coupled to a human, who also had a filing cabinet handy, then there is no trouble in asking that person how much the phone cost.

We are going to create little people handling the activities of all these otherwise dumb objects.

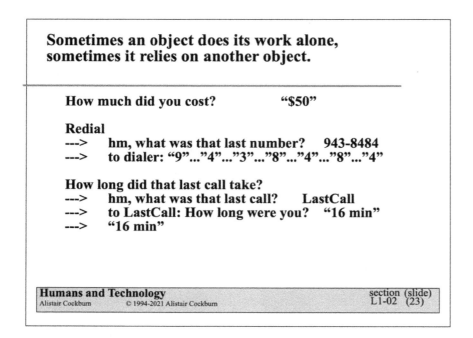

Staying with the bureaucracy, it makes sense that the person babysitting the phone wouldn't know certain things. The person babysitting the phone should know its cost and its number. But that person maybe shouldn't know the mechanics of making clicks or tones for dialing a number.

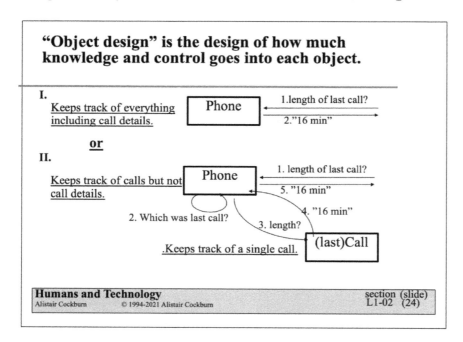

Here we see that the phone itself *could* but need not keep track of the details of each call. That would likely be the job of a person babysitting a "phone call" object. The call object (and its babysitter) would properly know what number was called and how long the call was.

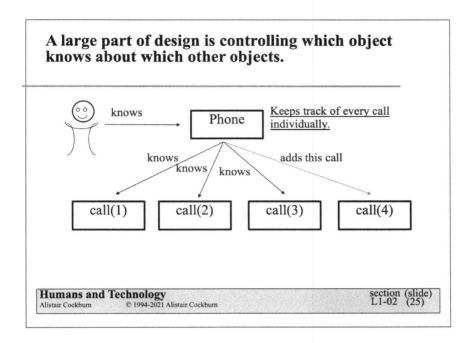

And that's the design assignment right there: Does the phone (and its babysitter) literally keep track of all the phone numbers dialed, the length of each call, and whatever else we want to know about them, or do we create a new object called a "call", have each "call" keep track of only their own one call details.

There is an added complexity in adding this new object, "call", but there is also nice bureaucratic tidiness in the separation of responsibilities. (The phone person says, "It's not *my* job to keep track of how long each those calls was we made over the last two months. Ask the calls themselves!")

That's really everything you need to know about object-oriented design. All the rest of the course, and really all of my design work personally, is just building off this bureaucracy design idea. Amazing how well it works.

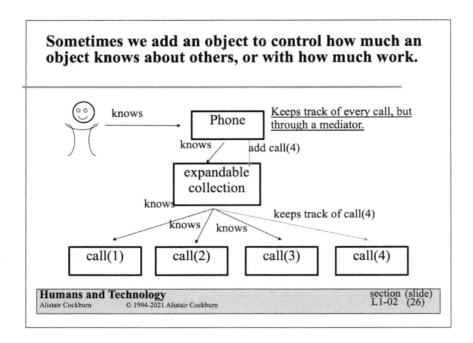

In slide 26 we see how objects beget new objects. The bureaucracy grows, as do all bureaucracies. The question is when to stop.

(Note for the skeptic: Yes, that expandable collection really is in there. It is so natural to you by now that you don't even think about adding it. Think about how hard your programming life would be if the phone had to create a separate variable for each new phone call!)

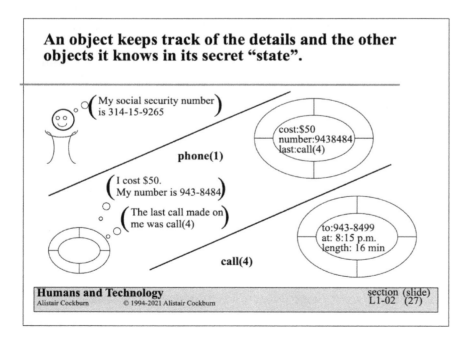

One of the fun things about 1994 was that we drew objects as donuts, with data on the inside and services around the outside. I don't know where this came from, I learned this from Chamond

Liu at IBM around 1990 and still prefer to draw objects this way.

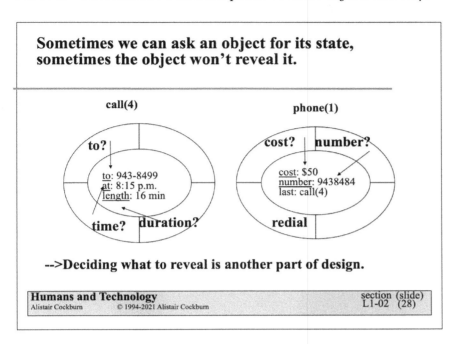

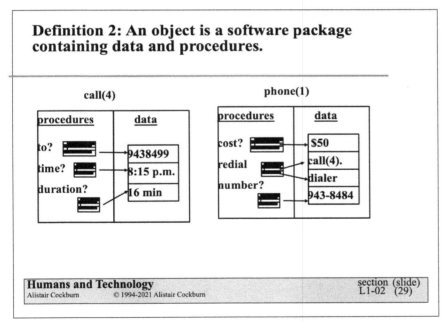

Here, for the programmers in the class, I finally show how the donut picture maps to storage in the computer. Each object has two spaces, one for the procedures and one for the data. Notice that the phone has in its data a reference to call(4) so that the phone can ask the call for its information. Note also that we have already started to have the call keep track of more information (the time of the call), so probably it was a good thing to pull the call out as a separate object from the phone.

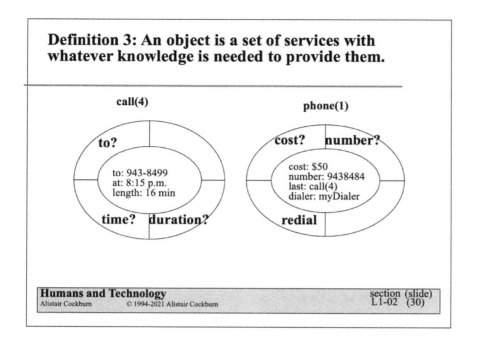

This may look like the same as the earlier slides and definition, but there is a linguistic shift to what I call "design from the outside", where the speaking about an object is focused on what services it provides, and the internal data-keeping is made a deferred topic. Design discussions then focus on what services objects provide each other, rather than what data they hold. This is a subtle shift that affects designs and design discussions profoundly.

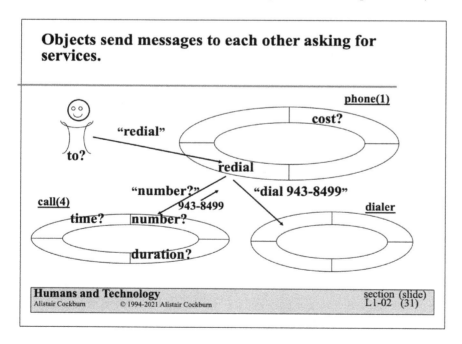

In the design discussions, the designers can just ask, "Should it know that or get help for that?" This simplifies the design discussions.

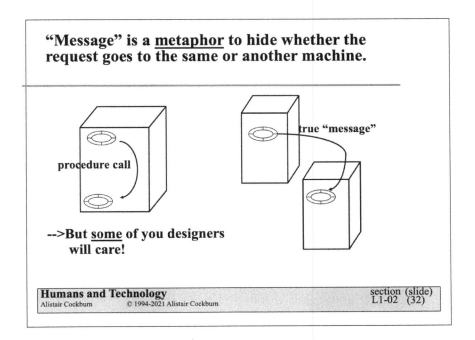

The final part of this module is to introduce the word "message" as part of our vocabulary. In 1994 we did not yet have service-oriented architectures (and the message idea was invented in the early 1970s, twenty years earlier!), so it was more metaphorical than real. However, the point was that we really wouldn't care whether another object was in the in same compiled file or on a distributed server in the cloud, we just had a request for information or action.

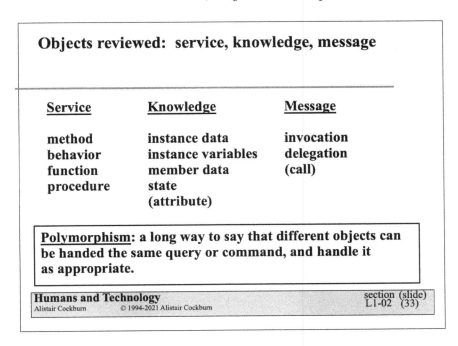

I don't think I spent much time on this slide, it is just a listing of different words being used.

A benefit of Object is it provides the designer the spectrum from all data to all behavior.

The average object has some data, some procedure.

A "Value" is data that must be associated. together.
- similar to a "data structure"
- e.g. a date, a check.

A "Script" is mostly behavior.
- like a procedure or rule base

Objects allows the designer to choose the amount of data and the amount of behavior.

Humans and Technology
Alistair Cockburn   © 1994-2021 Alistair Cockburn

section (slide)
L1-02 (34)

A hazard to beginners is to model "functions" as objects, when they should be services of objects.

A function can be a legitimate object.
  e.g.: multiplication, transferring money.

An object <u>should</u> have State and Services
  - what is the state of the transfer?
  - checkpoint the multiplication!

Experienced developers know how to discover functions.
  e.g.: printing

Beware functions (services) masquerading as objects!
  Hint: does it have more than 1 service ?

Humans and Technology
Alistair Cockburn   © 1994-2021 Alistair Cockburn

section (slide)
L1-02 (35)

The years since 1994 have been filled with arguments about just how much data and how much function objects should have. Pure data objects have a periodic resurgence, and functions as objects have a place. The cool thing about OO design is that it allows the full spectrum.

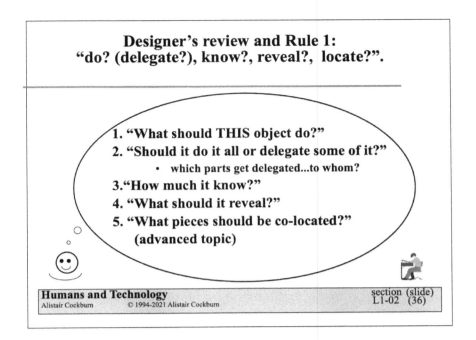

That wraps up the first module of designing with objects, using just the idea of objects as having babysitters working in a bureaucracy and calling on each other to help out with an assignment.

What is truly amazing is how well this works.

I was once teaching to class of beginners, and two people at one table were producing a really lovely design - they had the bureaucracy neatly sorted. I stopped by to ask them how they were doing that. It turned out they were FBI agents. One of them pointed to a card on the table and said, "That object has no *need to know* about that information." :) So good.

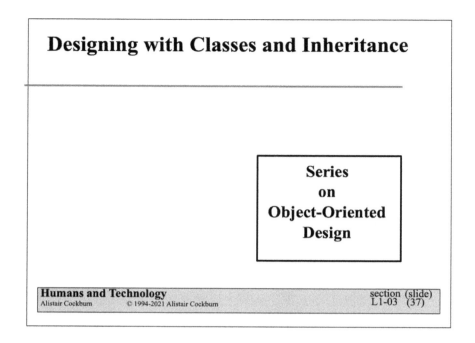

Inheritance adds power to the design but also danger.

In the mid-1990s, inheritance was considered the defining property of object-oriented languages, not polymorphism, as I presented in the "OO's Difference" lecture, and not the data-plus-services idea. As a consequence, inheritance usually got an overabundance of attention, which took the industry decades to shed.

My boss at IBM in the early 1990s was Wayne Stevens, one of creators of structured design back in the 1970s. He loved hated inheritance in object technology. He made it his goal - including using me - to stamp OO programming off the face of the earth, quite literally! He said it was carcinogenic and had terrible maintenance properties and I had to help him stamp it out. That's another long story. History has proven him partially right, although not completely.

We rely on inheritance in frameworks we use all the time, to simplify our work and reduce the knowledge we need to get things done. On our project in 1994, when we were done, one of the client's better programmers came on to add some functions. He was shocked at how little code he had to write to add it. He was expecting several weeks of work, and got done in days.

At the same time, in the games industry there is an entire architectural style that minimizes (I don't know if it totally eliminates) inheritance, for exactly the maintenance difficulties that Wayne Stevens recognized.

Let's see how I taught it back then.

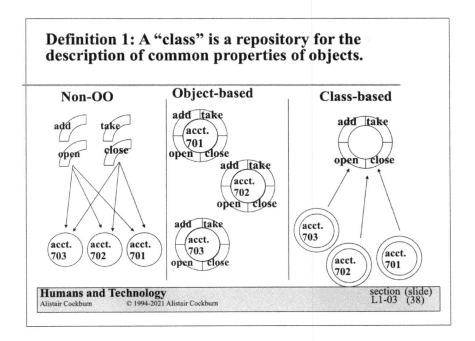

Definition 1: A "class" is a repository for the description of common properties of objects.

In the early days of working out what was this "object-oriented" thing, Brown University professor Peter Wegner wrote an paper in which he categorized languages as having objects, having classes, and having inheritance. He called them object-based, class-based, and object-oriented, in that order. Notice that polymorphism didn't make it into his categorization.

In 1990, I was writing in Prolog after having prototyped my system in Smalltalk. Missing my objects, I created an "object-based" system, very much as discussed in the previous module. I had to roll my own polymorphic switcher - the famous little blue box in the first lecture - and maintaining that nearly killed me. So I had come to really value polymorphism in the system. Wegner never said anything about polymorphism, for whatever reason.

A "class-based" system just had the facility for creating new objects of the same type. We would need that in the previous module's telephone example, to create all those "call" objects.

This slide shows how you would used abstract data types (on the left), just straight objects (the middle) and how the system could simplify things if all the procedures for the same kind of objects were just kept in one place.

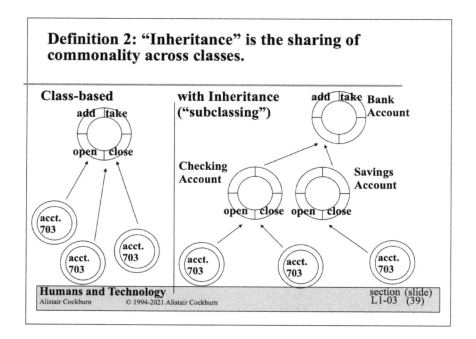

This book is not a tutorial on object-oriented programming, so I won't try to repeat the lecture. Presumably you already know what inheritance is and how it works. What this slide is showing is how one can minimize the work to be done by factoring out all the common parts of similar objects and putting those common parts into a central place.

What we have to investigate is how this changes the discussion about design, in particular, what to factor out and what to leave separate.

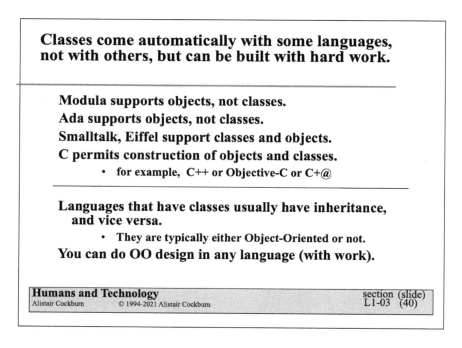

This is just the Wegner categorization being shown.

"Inheritance" in the problem space does not necessarily match inheritance in the design space.

Is a rectangle a subclass or a square, or vice versa, or what?

An insurance company has 23 variations of a kind of life insurance. Are there 23 subclasses?

Is there a mapping between problem-space classification and design-space subclassing?

Humans and Technology
Alistair Cockburn   © 1994-2021 Alistair Cockburn

section (slide)
L1-03   (41)

At this point, we open up the entire can of worms about inheritance. My point would be that once again, there are many ways to describe or model the world, and what we would want to ask is "What will help our maintenance and evolution of the system?"

Incidentally, I wrote an entire paper about that miserable square-rectangle riddle. Nobody would publish it, because it attacked a sacred cow, but the experts did quietly agree that it was correct. I actually enjoyed the writing of this paper, take a look: "Constructive deconstruction of subtyping" (https://web.archive.org/web/20140329202842/http://alistair.cockburn.us/Constructive+deconstruction+of+subtyping)

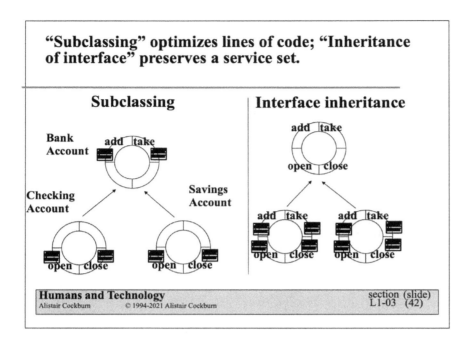

At this point, the design topics are getting increasingly subtle, and hard for beginners, but what I wanted to open up was the consideration of designing to minimize coding versus that idea of "design from the outside". In a design from the outside, we care that things behave the same way, but don't mind repeating the code.

As with all design things, there are times for each. The practitioner just needs to learn to think about them.

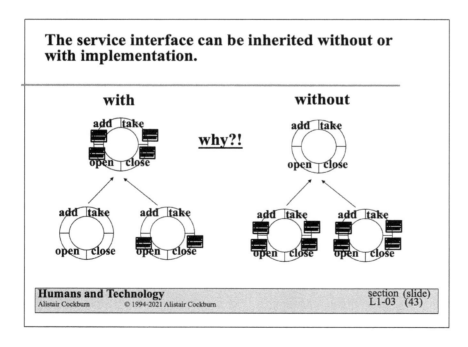

32

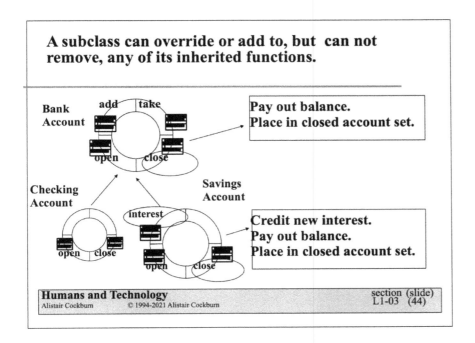

Basics of inheritance. Showing how a savings account is different from a simple bank account. You already know this stuff.

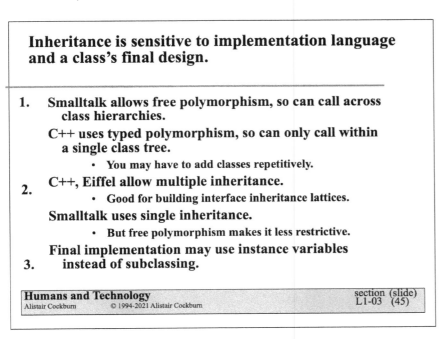

Because this was an introductory course, we didn't get into all of the variations and differences of all the languages. It was sufficient that the students would see that there were differences, and those differences would drive different designs.

Rule of Design: Identify classes early, but leave inheritance to language-specific class design.

1. **Identify which classes are needed.**
2. **Identify commonality between classes.**
3. **Let the class designer decide how best to implement the commonality**
   - Interface inheritance
   - Subclassing
   - Instance data

Humans and Technology
Alistair Cockburn   © 1994-2021 Alistair Cockburn

section (slide)
L1-03 (46)

Recalling that this was a course intended for business analysts and programmers alike, the important point I wanted to make here was that the final selection of inheritance details to use would rest with the programmer wrestling with performance and maintenance questions. No one design would be "intrinsically correct" over many of its near neighbors.

What I was after was that the business experts and the programmers could sensibly dialog together over what was "correct" in a business sense, and what was "good" for programming, and not get lost between those two.

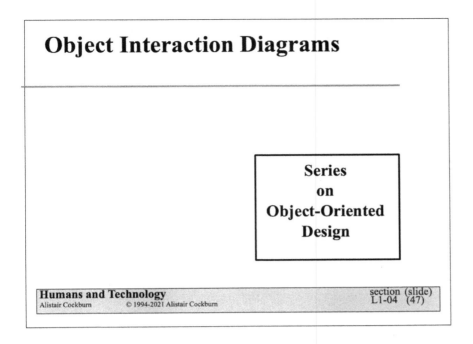

This module is a bit of an interlude. It was a good time to introduce the different ways of showing how objects interact with each other, and how those drawings would support the design discussions.

As is my usual mode, I found the unifying principle across different diagramming styles, and showed them as different projections of the same thing.

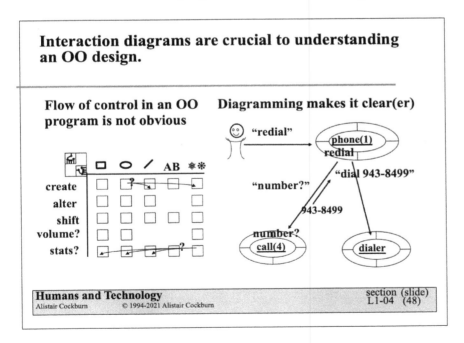

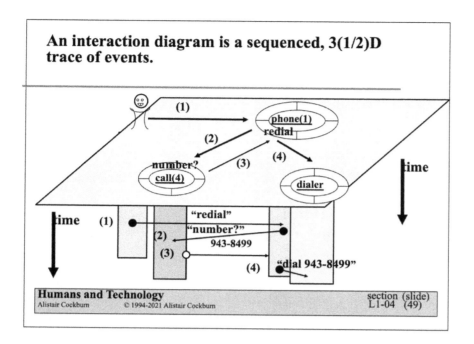

Here's the unifying view. We have on the top plane the drawings from before, with the message sequence labeled. It is possible to show time going down the page, in which case the messages don't have to be numbered. With this 3D view, we see how we can choose which projection suits our purpose.

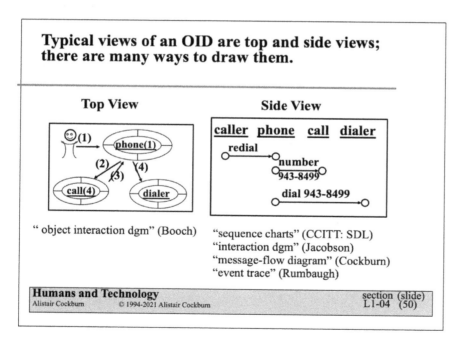

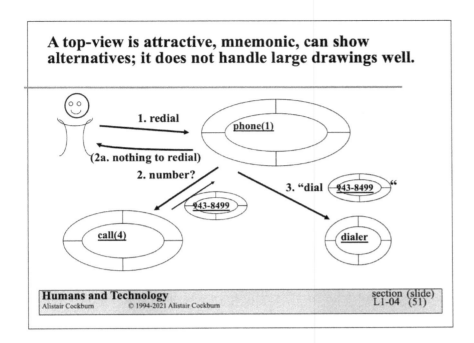

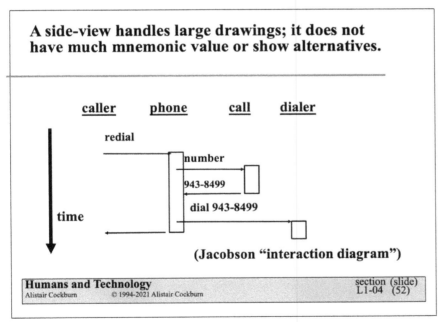

As a little historical note, I spent 1987-1991 at IBM Research in Switzerland deeply understanding these side-view diagrams. Our team did some early AI work making it so the IBM network protocol designers could start sketching ideas for a network protocol with these diagrams, and our system would interpret the sketches as they were drawn and build the protocol definition from those. It was fun and rigorous at the same time, and ended up in a small number of obscure papers like "Formalizing Temporal Message-Flow Diagrams". (https://dblp.org/rec/conf/pstv/Cockburn91.html and https://onlinelibrary.wiley.com/doi/abs/10.1002/spe.4380251205). As as result, I know much too much about these things. :)

OID are called sequence charts, event traces, message flow diagrams, and are drawn in numerous styles.

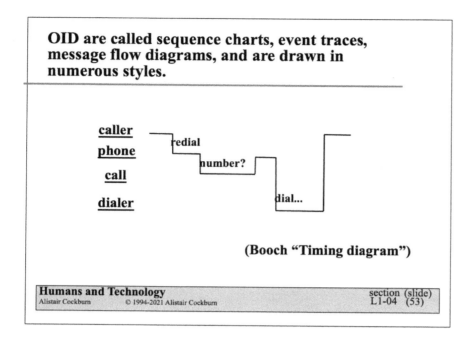

(Booch "Timing diagram")

Use whatever your tools support. Top views for small documentation, side views for traces.

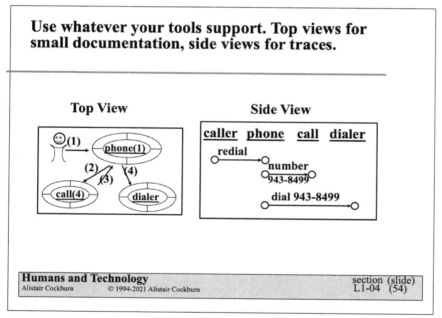

And as always, use whichever suits the needs of the moment.

We'll see more of both types throughout the course.

There have been studies on formalizing OIDs, none yet suited for program development

But, you can imagine some code generation from OIDs, and use of trace visualization tools...

...soon to arrive at a vendor near you.

Humans and Technology
Alistair Cockburn   © 1994-2021 Alistair Cockburn

section (slide)
L1-04 (55)

Yeah, I wrote that in 1994, still haven't seen them.

Humans and Technology
Alistair Cockburn   © 1994-2021 Alistair Cockburn

section (slide)
L1-04 (56)

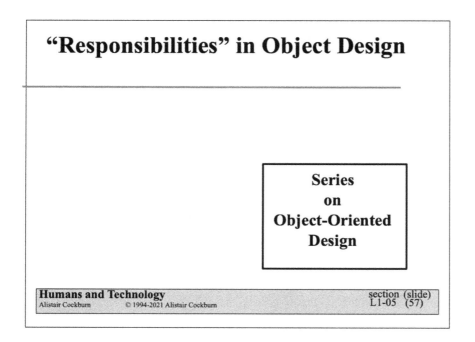

The final module in the design question, "responsibilities" tie the design ideas together.

Since "responsibilities" are written for the humans and are not executable, they got left out by most design tool designers. As a result, even when we wanted to mark the responsibilities for our classes, most tools literally had no place for us to put them. And so they didn't get used on live projects, which is a shame.

Ward Cunningham and Kent Beck first wrote about using responsibilities in their 1989 OOPSLA paper "A laboratory for teaching object-oriented thinking" (http://www.cs.unc.edu/~stotts/COMP145/CRC/papers/beck.html). In there they write:

"A responsibility serves as a handle for discussing potential solutions. The responsibilities of an object are expressed by a handful of short verb phrases, each containing an active verb. The more that can be expressed by these phrases, the more powerful and concise the design."

Rebecca Wirfs-Brock and her co-authors developed the responsibilities idea into a full-blown design methodology called responsibility-driven design in their 1990 book *Designing Object-Oriented Software* and the 2002 update, *Object Design: Roles, Responsibilities, and Collaborations*.

I learned these design techniques from their papers, workshops and in conversations. Eventually I wrote my own technique guides, "Using CRC Cards" and "Responsibility-Based Modeling" (as with this course, intended for business people as well as programmers). Who knows, I might around to publishing those as monographs one day.

Each unit in a system plays a role... it has a "responsibility" to the functioning of the system.

(This is always true, not just for Object-Orientation)

"Responsibility" was coined by Ward Cunningham and Kent Beck to describe essence of good OO designs.

Naming and allocating responsibilities is key to design.
  -> determines system decomposition and flow.

Humans and Technology
Alistair Cockburn   © 1994-2021 Alistair Cockburn   section (slide) L1-05 (58)

An object can delegate to others, calling upon their responsibilities.

"Design with responsibilities" mirrors society,
So...
1. Pretend you were the object...
2. Ask yourself, "Is it really my responsibility to handle this?"
3. Ask, "Who would I call upon to help, who has the responsibility to help in that way?"
4. (Practice different scenarios to stress-test the allocation of responsibilities.)

Humans and Technology
Alistair Cockburn   © 1994-2021 Alistair Cockburn   section (slide) L1-05 (59)

Here we are, back with Weber's bureaucracies' "It's not my job" and the FBI agents' "Do they have a need to know?". People are just so good at these two questions that they very naturally come up with partitions that make good sense and also pretty good initial designs.

A unit's role or responsibility can usually be stated in one or two short phrases.

"Knows about collecting money and giving change."
- Coffee machine coin/credit collection unit

"Knows its business purpose and mediates its business attributes."
- Generic statement for a business object.
- It does not claim to know how the data is stored.

"Knows how the data for a particular business object is stored."
- A "data broker" object for the business object.

"Knows and controls the details of a transaction."
- Transaction object (e.g. a Withdrawal)

Humans and Technology   section (slide)
Alistair Cockburn   © 1994-2021 Alistair Cockburn   L1-05 (60)

Responsible for writing the methodology to be used on the IBM Consulting Group's OO projects in the early and mid-1990s, including coding standards and design guidelines, I learned that not everything can be stated tidily in just one short phrase. Sometimes two, or occasionally three are needed. Not everyone is this permissive in their guidelines, some people insist that it must fit into one short phrase. However, my goal is to impose as few restrictions on people as possible and still get decent outcomes. Hence "one or two short phrases."

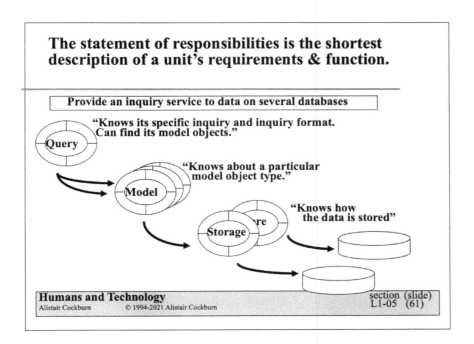

This is the point exactly: "The statement of responsibilities is the shortest description of a unit's requirements and function."

Discussing possible design ideas, partitions, objects, interactions, data, behavior is complicated. There is a lot to keep track of. Inside those discussions, one can move more quickly if there is capsule-summary at hand of what an object's about.

My main design heuristic then, and still now, is:

"Do the object's name, responsibility-statement, and service/data details all line up?"

Over time the design idea shifts and drifts, and it can turn out that one of the three is no longer in alignment. It's not a given which of the three is wrong (it could be just the name needs to be updated). Having just the name and the services/data details isn't sufficient to tell if they are out of whack, because we are missing the *intention* of the designer. The responsibility statement shows that intention.

This is why it is so sad that the tools don't support the inclusion of the responsibility statement.

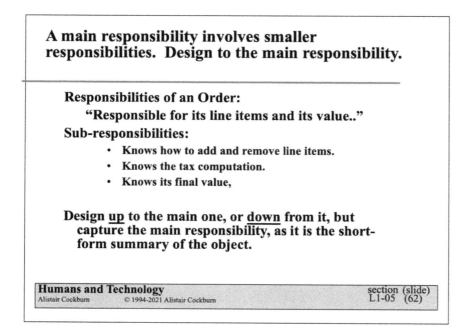

Responsibilities are recursive, of course. But that's not really confusing, we do this all the time in normal talking. The goal is to find a fairly short phrase that capture the intention of the name given (or which allows a good name to be chosen).

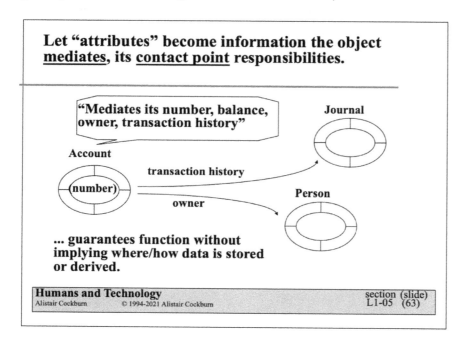

"Contact point responsibilities" is a nice phrase, matching the bureaucracy model: "Who would I call who can put me in contact with the right person?" -- and then we expect that mediator person to bow out of the conversation. Bureaucracy is a powerful tool for design thinking. :)

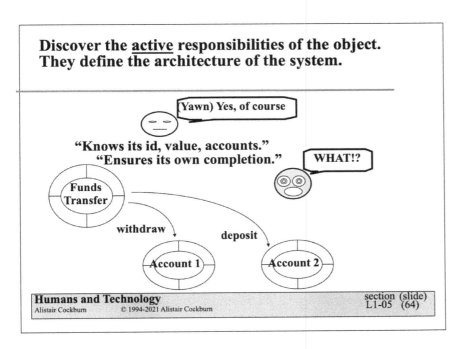

What I learned in the early 1990s that still is true is that it is easy just to name a bunch of data to babysit, but doing so doesn't convey much of what is going on. Active verbs tell a lot with a little.

Plus, I like that big-eyed red face. It will show up again :)

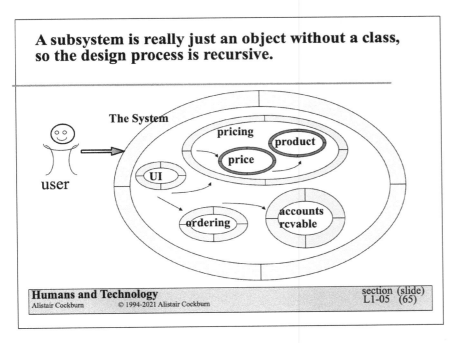

Since a computer, a module, a subsystem is an "object," not with classes or inheritance, all the design discussion we've done up to here still applies. This is great, since it allows us to break a giant system up into sensible parts, and keep breaking down from there.

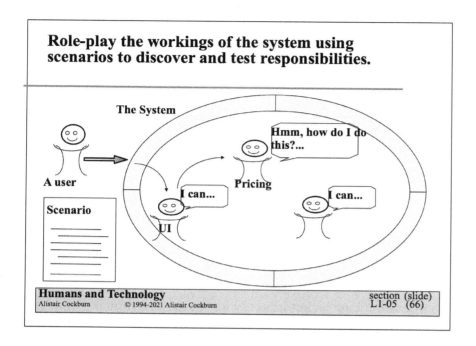

Part of the CRC-card technique is to walk through different scenarios in succession, to test and to spark changes to the responsibilities allocation. This breaks the log jam the old database designers in the 1990s ran into: when to stop modeling the details of the business. The answer is: only model enough to run the scenarios.

The entire following module is about designing with scenarios.

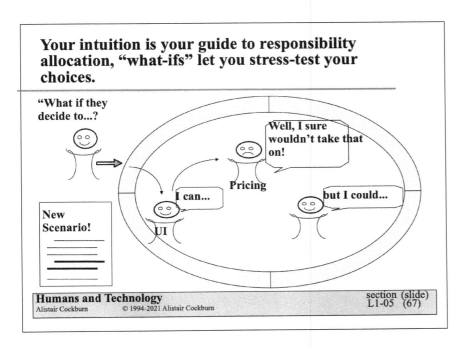

It is really amazing how well our daily intuition guides us in "that name doesn't match that responsibility", "it's not my job", "get that person/thing out of the middle of that conversation", and so on.

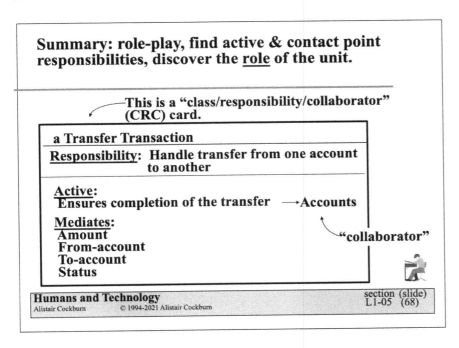

We used these "Class-Responsibility-Collaborator" cards to quickly revise and cycle through possible designs. By this point you should be able to read what's on that card and do similarly for your own system. Try it.

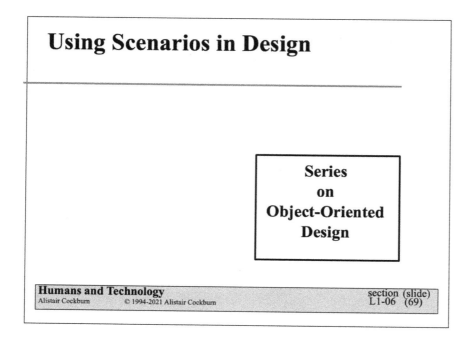

Looking at these slides now, I find it interesting how I slide into use cases starting from shifting designs around using different scenarios. In this module, we continue with that, but also get a little formal about just what to write in a scenario and how to collect them. From there the jump to use cases is pretty easy.

Odd, I haven't taught in this sequence since the late 1990s, when I would go straight into use case structure. This sequence here makes good sense, though, because nobody started the conversation by asking "What is a use case?" It started with "How do I design a system?" Getting to use cases as a writing format is natural as a late-stage topic here. Fascinating.

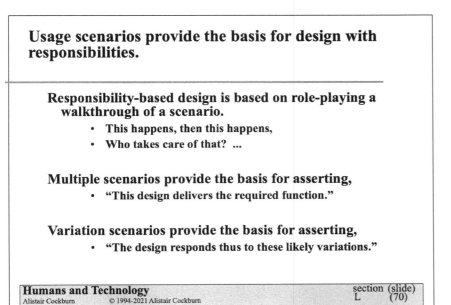

This is just a recap of the previous module.

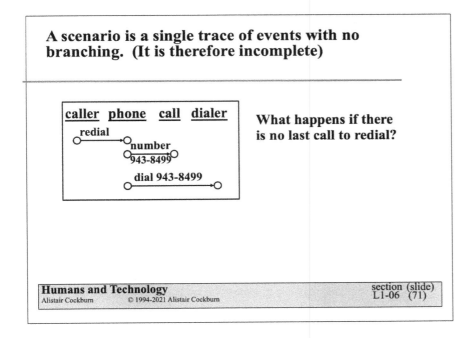

This is a critical definition of a scenario: that it has no branching. It's just a sequence. We'll come back to this later.

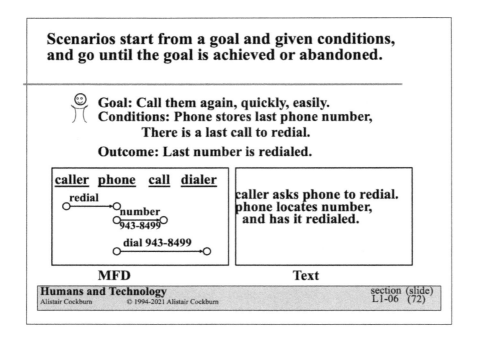

This is the first time that "goals" and "outcomes" show up. We debated so much in those days what an object's responsibilities were if it couldn't carry out it's service promise. For example, suppose you are going somewhere in a taxi and it gets a flat tire. What is the taxi driver's responsibility to you? Charge you for the distance driven? Get you a new taxi? Nothing?

For an object in a computer system, what are it's responsibilities if the network goes down or the power goes out? Sometimes it's nothing, sometimes it's not nothing. Which subsystem, module or object carries that load?

These are perplexing questions, which nonetheless have to be answered for a system design.

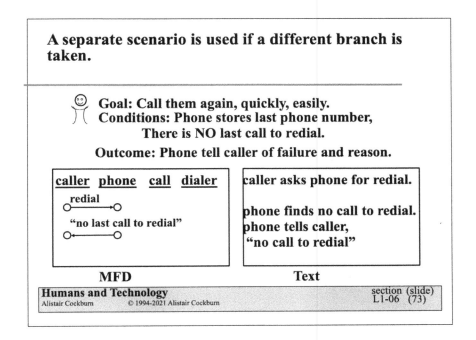

In playing with CRC cards, we usually don't write down the specific scenarios, things are moving too fast. Here I am slowly formalizing the topic of goal, scenario conditions and outcome. Largely, I'm trying to get the students to slow down their thinking for a moment and notice what they are doing intuitively. We'll build on that later.

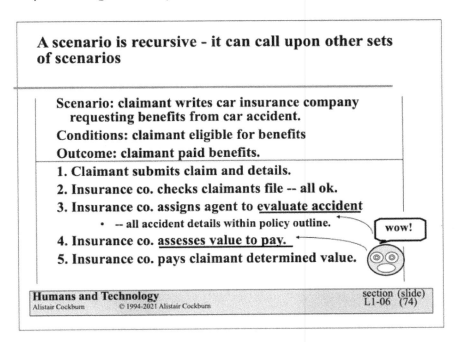

Ah, my red-faced friend. Hyperlinking wasn't so very common in 1994, although Lotus Notes had it (which we used in our use cases). Once again, in ordinary speaking and writing we use the recursive nature of goals, actions, verbs to bundle details. People need really little coaching to see "assess value to pay" as a scenario to be written about elsewhere.

We underlined those verb phrases that would be described elsewhere, then it turned out that when hyperlinks in documents came along, they map perfectly and supports this natural, recursive style of presentation.

It kind of blows my mind that we were doing this in 1994. AOL gave me my first web site late in 1994 (don't laugh), and for sure we had hyperlinks there. But they weren't common in documents at the time.

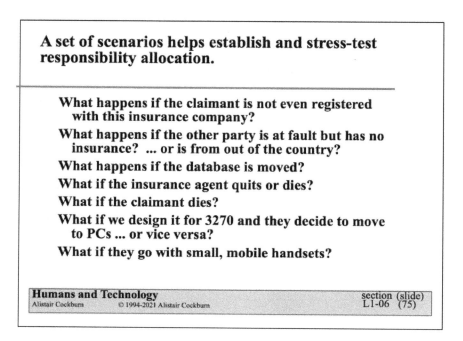

A set of scenarios helps establish and stress-test responsibility allocation.

What happens if the claimant is not even registered with this insurance company?

What happens if the other party is at fault but has no insurance? ... or is from out of the country?

What happens if the database is moved?

What if the insurance agent quits or dies?

What if the claimant dies?

What if we design it for 3270 and they decide to move to PCs ... or vice versa?

What if they go with small, mobile handsets?

Humans and Technology
Alistair Cockburn   © 1994-2021 Alistair Cockburn

section (slide)
L1-06 (75)

While you're running through scenarios in a CRC-card session, it is good to brainstorm all the things that can go wrong. These eventually need to all go into the requirements document and test cases.

It doesn't matter if the requirements writers get there first and write them down in the requirements document, or the testers get there first and write them down in the test cases, or the designers get there first (and probably don't write them down at all), eventually all of the oddball cases have to be considered. Ideally, though not usually, those oddball cases get run through a responsibilities simulation to check that the design is still holding up well and feeling right.

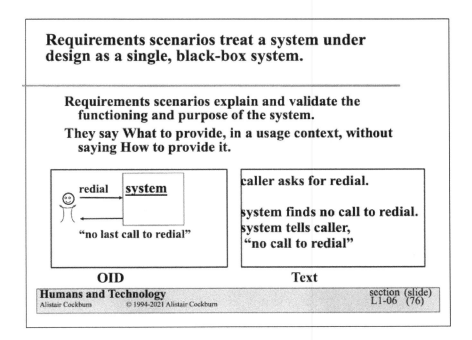

We see here the concept of black-box design and writing requirements for black-boxes showing up for the first time. Again, this is natural - we just need to requirement people to only say the word "system" as opposed to naming parts of the system, and the language just flows out naturally.

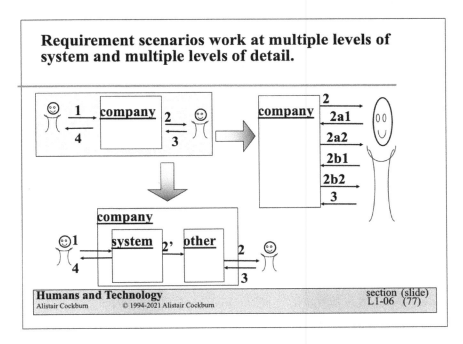

Repeating yet again something that is natural in ordinary language but gets forgotten so fast in systems discussions: You can control what level of system, what level of disclosure you use at any moment, and in this way, control the complexity of the discussion. It also allows you to defer design topics to other teams doing subsystem design.

Include scenarios of use for every user of the system -- include test and maintenance!!

Identify the actors who will use the system
   Actors may be people, computers, programs,
   end users, maintenance personnel, testers.
Make test and maintenance standard actors!

Humans and Technology
Alistair Cockburn   © 1994-2021 Alistair Cockburn

section (slide)
L1-06 (78)

LOL. How we forget maintenance activities :).

Summarize functional requirements in 4-columns: actor, goal, system responsibility, data needs.

ATM actor	goal	system responsibility	data needs
account owner	withdraw money	give $, receipt; update balance	acct #, code, amount.
bank employee	refill cash drawer	update cash balance.	$ amount.
maintenance staff	refill paper	register paper (non)empty	paper present.
tester	test many situations	read/run test scripts, & produce report.	test scripts.
installer	initialize system	reset to start state.	"initialize" signal.

Humans and Technology
Alistair Cockburn   © 1994-2021 Alistair Cockburn

section (slide)
L1-06 (79)

This is interesting for me to see now. I use that 4-column table to summarize use cases. I didn't recall that we had done that with scenarios, too. I suspect I was just setting up for the lecture on use cases.

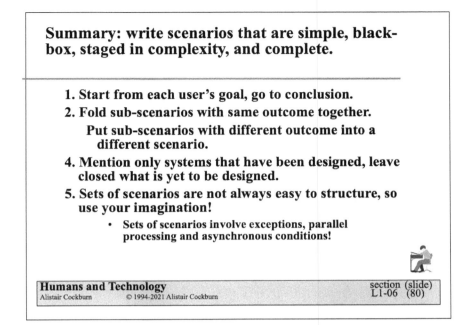

Summary: write scenarios that are simple, black-box, staged in complexity, and complete.

1. Start from each user's goal, go to conclusion.
2. Fold sub-scenarios with same outcome together.

   Put sub-scenarios with different outcome into a different scenario.
4. Mention only systems that have been designed, leave closed what is yet to be designed.
5. Sets of scenarios are not always easy to structure, so use your imagination!
   - Sets of scenarios involve exceptions, parallel processing and asynchronous conditions!

Humans and Technology
Alistair Cockburn   © 1994-2021 Alistair Cockburn

section (slide)
L1-06   (80)

Definitely setting all the building blocks in place to step into the use cases discussion.

Probably the most unusual thing I see here in hindsight is the attention to a goal having a particular outcome, and that the scenario should run up to that outcome. Relevant for use cases, coming right up, just interesting for me to see that here with the scenarios.

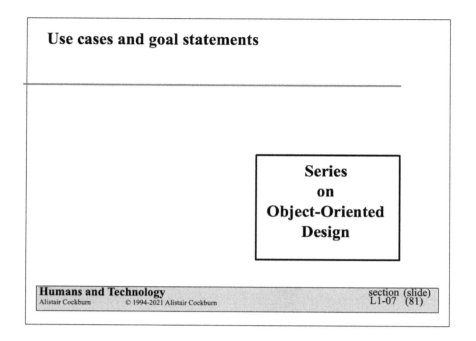

Use cases were invented by Ivar Jacobson in the 1980s. He told me that he wanted to collect together all the related possibilities together in a packet, what lawyers call a "case". In Swedish, "användningsfall", or "case of usage". Recognizing that that funny phrase would have no marketability in English, he shortened it to "use case."

If you come into a class on use cases, you ask, "What is a use case?" and the teacher has to develop the thinking from there. In this class, though, we are discussing *design*. We have already covered responsibilities and designing with scenarios. We already have scenarios marked with the user's intention and the outcome. All we have to do now is sew them together.

It took almost two years for me to understand a set of things that Ivar probably understood intuitively but never articulated, without which use cases were confusing:

- All scenarios are collected together by the users' *goals* they support.
- Goals have sub-goals, so goals are recursive. They operate at different levels related to how long they take to achieve, from seconds to years.
- Recursive is confusing. Goal levels need to be tagged in order that the reader doesn't get confused.
- Both "system/module/object" and "goal/scenario/use case" are recursive, so now the writing drifts everywhere. I tagged the critical goal level as "what the user wants to finish in this one sitting" (a *task-level* goal) and the system design level as "the exact system or application *this team* has to design". Tagging those two levels prevented the writing from drifting all over the place.

Making these ideas explicit allowed me to teach people how to write use cases in a repeatable way. I wrote the ideas in an article in 1994, elaborated in the book *Writing Effective Use Cases*. The early reviewers of the book wrote, "Now the riddle of use cases is solved." :)

A "use case" is a group of requirements scenarios with two outcomes: goal attained or abandoned.

Describes usage of the system - context for the "why".
  "Why are we requiring this function?"
Shows the intention of a key user: their <u>goal</u>.
System may be able to deliver goal or not (conditions)
Use case covers
  0. goal delivered without problem,
  1. goal delivered after failure recovery,
  2. goal abandoned.

Humans and Technology
Alistair Cockburn   © 1994-2021 Alistair Cockburn

section (slide)
L1-07 (82)

This notion of a goal being abandoned is weird, we are not used to it, especially not in requirements or process description documents. It is the essence of why a use case is different from a scenario, though.

Think of the taxi driver again. The taxi driver can get us to the airport; or can have a breakdown and call another taxi, who gets us to the airport; or just tells us we have to find our own way there. The use case is the place where we collect together all of these scenarios.

A use case is characterized by actor and goal. It contains scenarios.

An actor is a person, computer or other active thing.
"What is the actor trying to accomplish?"
"What scenarios can occur in pursuing this goal?"
  Both success and failure scenarios.
Examples:
  Operator wants to find desired music selection.
  Owner wants to withdraw money from bank.
  Customer wants to trade money for goods.
  Customer wants to register change of address.

Humans and Technology
Alistair Cockburn   © 1994-2021 Alistair Cockburn

section (slide)
L1-07 (83)

A use case has success and failure outcomes, a scenario has only one outcome.

Primary Actor: Account owner Primary Actor's Goal: withdraw money			Use case characteristic information
Knows codes, Has funds.	Knows codes, No funds here, Other funds.	Knows codes, Not sufficient funds anywhere	Scenario conditions
Presses button.	Presses button.	Presses button.	Trigger
Get codes. ok. Ask amount.ok. Give money.	Get codes. ok. Ask amount.Nok. Transfer funds. ok. Give money	Get codes. ok. Ask amount. Nok. Transfer funds. Fail. Refuse money.	Scenario steps
Succeed		Failure	Outcome

Humans and Technology
Alistair Cockburn   © 1994-2021 Alistair Cockburn
section (slide)
L1-07 (84)

Notice the formatting here: every scenario gets its own column. The top has the conditions, the rest of the column outlines the sequence particular to those conditions. This is still a use case, just with the scenarios listed separately. I encountered projects where they wrote the requirements this way. It is legitimate, but requires a lot of work when something changes. You have to change every column to match the new ideas. Tiring, and also error-prone. Ivar's technique of folding the scenarios together is a brilliant way of capturing all the scenarios with no duplication.

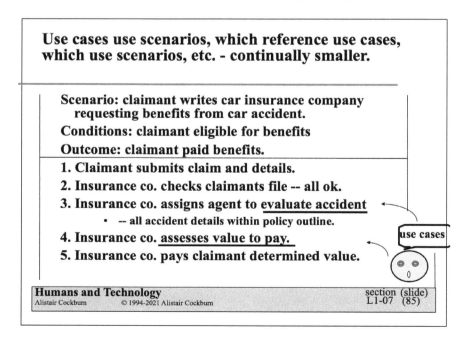

Use cases use scenarios, which reference use cases, which use scenarios, etc. - continually smaller.

Scenario: claimant writes car insurance company requesting benefits from car accident.

Conditions: claimant eligible for benefits

Outcome: claimant paid benefits.

1. Claimant submits claim and details.
2. Insurance co. checks claimants file -- all ok.
3. Insurance co. assigns agent to <u>evaluate accident</u>
   - -- all accident details within policy outline.
4. Insurance co. <u>assesses value to pay.</u>
5. Insurance co. pays claimant determined value.

use cases

Humans and Technology
Alistair Cockburn   © 1994-2021 Alistair Cockburn
section (slide)
L1-07 (85)

Now that we know goals can fail, "Evaluate accident" and "Assess value to pay" become references to other use cases, not just scenarios.

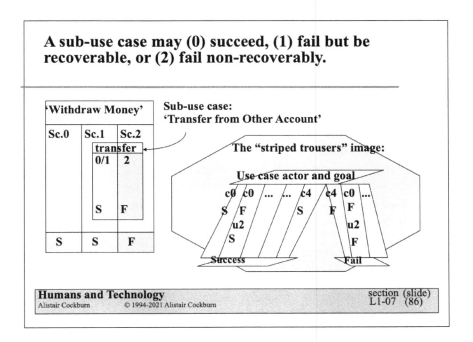

I love this striped pants metaphor. :) It's a cute way of illustrating that all of the scenarios are held together by the belt (the goal), and that a use case always has two terminations, the success and the failure. The little nested picture on the left shows how a lower-level use cases fold back into a higher-level use cases. All of the successes in the lower-level use case fold back into just one stripe (scenario) in the higher-level one, and all of the failures in the lower-level one fold into just one other stripe in the higher-level one. This prevents an explosion of scenarios when you combine higher- and lower-level ones. It's a sweet and unexpected outcome.

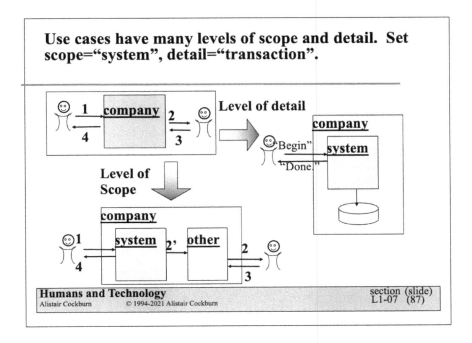

Here is the picture of the two different unfoldings of a use case: digging into the system being designed, opening it up into its component parts, and digging into the actions of the user at the outside *without* opening up the system into its component parts.

It was always hard to teach people that latter one, that you can put a magnifying glass on the actions without invading the design space of the item to be designed, just break open the interactions at the boundary.

This one slide doesn't really do justice to that topic. I spent years and years trying out different ways to clarify the two dimensions of expansion, none of them worked really well. It's just hard for people to handle those two, independent expansions. That's why I had people just focus on the *task* of the user, and the system under immediate design. I could then add the few other glue use cases that went up and down the levels.

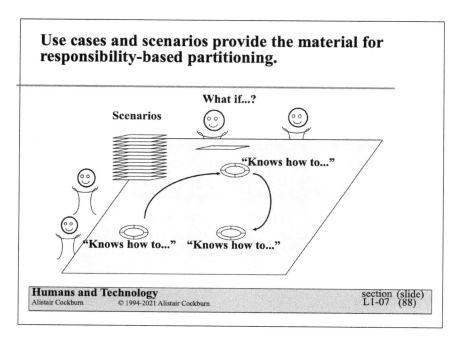

We literally did this on that project in 1994. To test the basic object model we had in front of us at the start of the project, we walked through a small but key set of use cases (not all of the 214 of them!), called out all the scenarios we could think of, and tested for holes in the design. The first one failed immediately :). Once we had a plausible object model that passed those tests, we accepted it as the base model. Periodically during the project, when we needed to poke into a design section, we would pull out the use cases and do the same, at a detailed level.

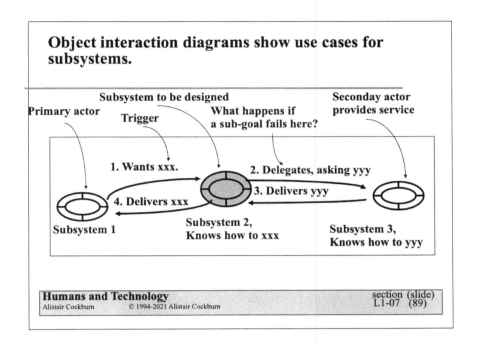

Object interaction diagrams show use cases for subsystems.

Subsystem to be designed · Primary actor · Trigger · What happens if a sub-goal fails here? · Seconday actor provides service

1. Wants xxx. · 2. Delegates, asking yyy · 3. Delivers yyy · 4. Delivers xxx

Subsystem 1 · Subsystem 2, Knows how to xxx · Subsystem 3, Knows how to yyy

Humans and Technology
Alistair Cockburn © 1994-2021 Alistair Cockburn
section (slide) L1-07 (89)

This is an idea which we didn't use much, but is plausible. Take a large system, do object-responsibility design to the subsystem level, and use that then as a spec for the subsystems.

Although fine in theory, I don't know that I have ever seen this done for real on a large project.

Summarize interface requirements in a table: use case, trigger, secondary actors, interface types.

use case	trigger	secondary actors	interface type
withdraw money	key press	bank central cash dispenser	database table. hot link.
refill cash drawer	lift $ sensor	cash dispenser	hot link
test many situations	program command	server computer	flat file.
initialize system	key press	none	- - -

Humans and Technology
Alistair Cockburn © 1994-2021 Alistair Cockburn
section (slide) L1-07 (90)

This is something we did do to bid that project. We had around 240 use cases, too much to read through and handle at one time. We created a spreadsheet with all the meta-information *about* the use cases, and then sorted and evaluated the spreadsheet. Not enough teams do this, it is really valuable.

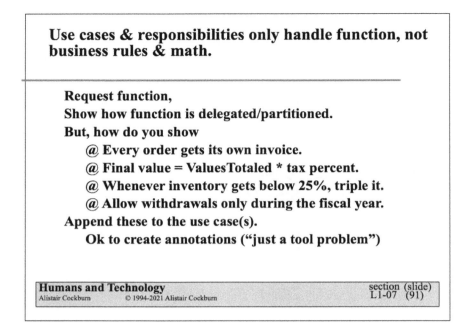

People get lost in writing use cases, and forget that they only capture a certain type of information: interactions with a limited amount of branchiness. I have found in my consulting that quite often when I go to a project to help them with their use cases, I tell them to write down what they are thinking in other formats: UI descriptions, tables, formulas, finite-state machines. Use cases are only one of the writing formats available to the team.

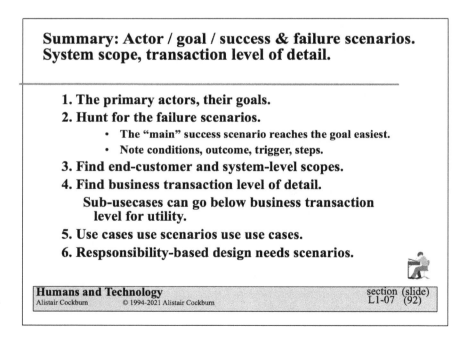

There's the roll-up. And yes, I see the typo, but this is literally the course as I taught it back then. Evidently, I had a typo. ;)

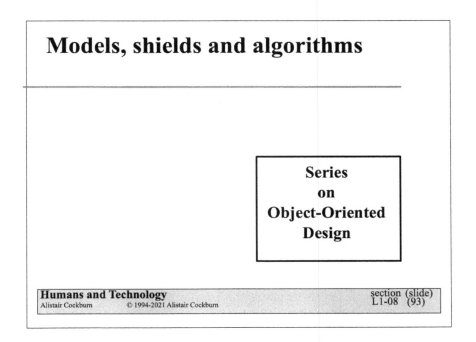

At this point we start jumping off to the more advanced topics. "Models and shields" was my nomenclature, I don't think it was popular or common in the rest of the industry.

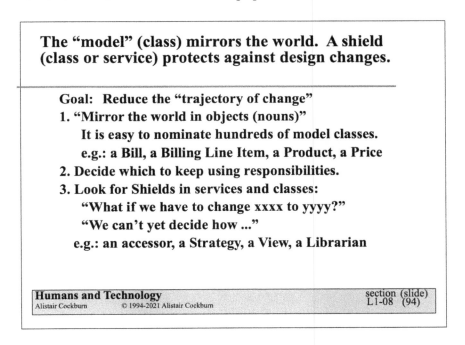

We were always asking ourselves: "Why are we doing this? What is it we really care about?" My conclusion was that when we do a good design, we benefit not just from the conceptual clarity, but that when it comes time to make a change, odds are in our favor that the changes are relatively localize, they don't stretch out all through our code. "Reduce the trajectory of change" is the phrase I chose for that. I still think this is the case.

A shield (service or class) provides an interface to allow variation.

Consider known "change cases" (John Bennett):
"We know this will change..."
"We don't know how it will be stored."
"We expect it eventually to be computed on the fly."
"Let's hard-code it in the prototype"
Shields protect your clients, reduce trajectory of change.
Scenarios / responsibilities help you find shields.
- A service lets you change <u>the</u> implementation
- A class lets you subclass for many implementations.

Humans and Technology
Alistair Cockburn   © 1994-2021 Alistair Cockburn
section (slide)
L1-08 (95)

There is an old adage in the programming: "*All problems can be solved with one more level of indirection.*" Every new function call or interface definition allows that additional level of indirection.

Introduce shield classes sparingly.

A shield class introduces complexity, delay.
e.g.: View classes as shields:
"External representations change often"...so
Separate the View from the Model
- Reuse same model using different views.
Now have View classes and Model classes.
- more complex but smaller changes
Resist temptation to introduce a "shield class" to avoid thinking!

Humans and Technology
Alistair Cockburn   © 1994-2021 Alistair Cockburn
section (slide)
L1-08 (96)

The benefit of adding yet-another function call, class, API, or level of inheritance is that it protects against future variations. The cost is cognitive and textual complexity. I found that beginners would get so excited about OO design options that they would be injecting inheritance, classes and function calls everywhere, to the point that you couldn't tell what was going on any more. Testing got more complicated, too, but mostly, the design complexity passed comprehension. I was fighting against that.

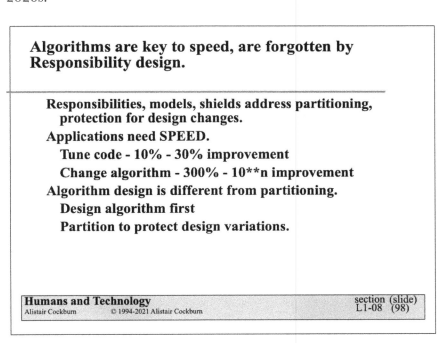

The best design makes Model objects Shields!

Good Shields ("Promotion") look like Models
   plus protect lots of future designs.
Look for generic business artifacts
After agonizing scrutiny and trial:
   <u>Video Rental co. has Promotions for Customers</u>
- What is the responsibility of a Video?
- of a Promotion?
- of a Movie?
- What kinds of Promotions?

Humans and Technology
Alistair Cockburn   © 1994-2021 Alistair Cockburn
   section (slide)
   L1-08 (97)

The early practitioners of Extreme Programming were masters of not introducing unnecessary inheritance, but finding valid domain concepts that encapsulated decisions neatly and provided the shield protection. Domain-Driven Development has carried these ideas forward into the 2020s.

Algorithms are key to speed, are forgotten by Responsibility design.

Responsibilities, models, shields address partitioning,
   protection for design changes.
Applications need SPEED.
   Tune code - 10% - 30% improvement
   Change algorithm - 300% - 10**n improvement
Algorithm design is different from partitioning.
   Design algorithm first
   Partition to protect design variations.

Humans and Technology
Alistair Cockburn   © 1994-2021 Alistair Cockburn
   section (slide)
   L1-08 (98)

Shifting away from our love for responsibilities, here is a reminder about other design factors. Typically, on a project only a few people actually spend time designing the key algorithms, and they should be sensitive to this topic. It was just a reminder that responsibilities aren't everything.

Improve data structures and algorithm exponents.

Data structures hide their algorithmic complexity
Linked list = O(n) Array = O(1)
Tables = O(n**2)   Naive graphs = O(n**3)
Program FIRST for design safety,
Measure LATER for bottlenecks
Change exponent at the bottlenecks.

Humans and Technology
Alistair Cockburn   © 1994-2021 Alistair Cockburn

section (slide)
L1-08   (99)

Most programmers have no idea what the cost complexity is of the data structures they use. At least back in 1994, programmers would tweak code forever, trying to eliminate a few lines of code (me raising my hand here!), and never notice that that code had no impact on total running time. Most time is consumed in just a few places. Finding and clearing those few places is time better spent, though not as much fun (my hand still up :).

Summary: Start with model classes, find shields to protect design choices, algorithms to get speed.

---

1. **Listen carefully for the concepts in your conversations.**
   The concepts become Model classes.
2. **Stress test the responsibilities with variations.**
   Place a Shield where you will create change.
   Look for subclass needs.
3. **Improve program speed by improving algorithms (exponent improvements).**

Humans and Technology
Alistair Cockburn   © 1994-2021 Alistair Cockburn

section (slide)
L1-08   (100)

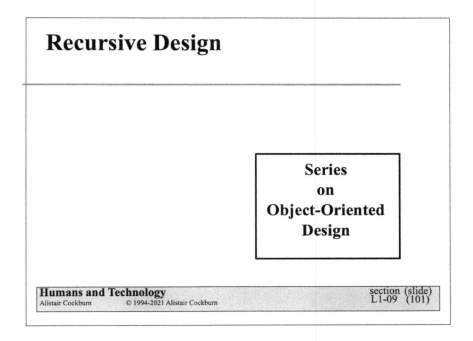

This module is really just a reminder of what we should already know, but putting together the ideas around starting from a big, hairy system and breaking it down into subsystems and components using the techniques we have already covered. There should be no surprises in here.

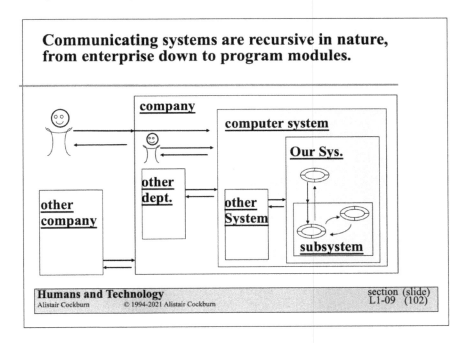

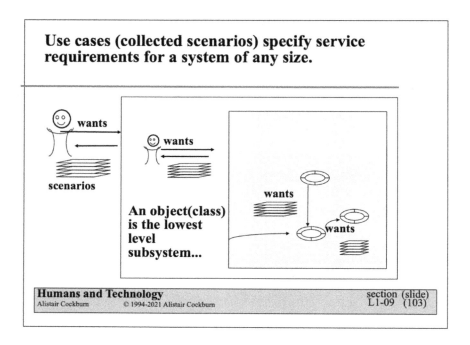

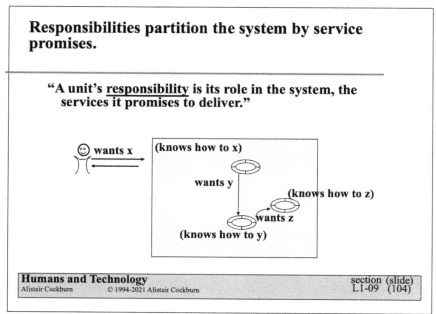

Just a little reminder here, that a subsystem is an "object" exactly as defined in the first module. So we can apply all of the design techniques for "object-based" design that we already know.

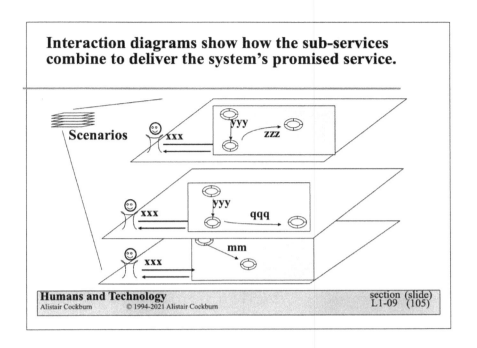

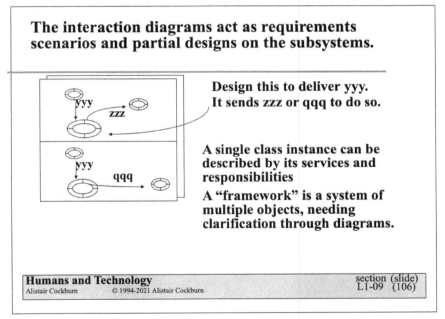

I have encountered projects where they did this. However, I didn't get to visit with those projects long enough to learn how happy they were with the results and whether they would work the same way again. So as far as I am concerned, it is still "interesting theory." It could work, but I don't know how well it works compared to other alternatives.

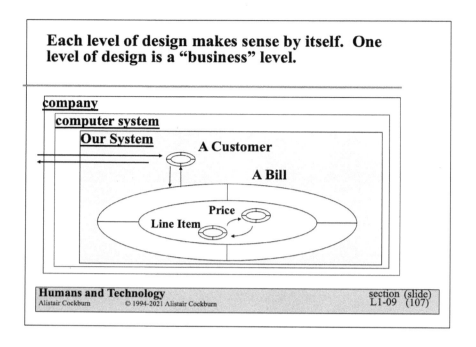

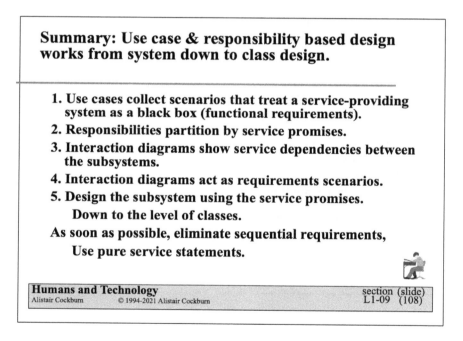

That's the end of design, folks! Nothing more to say on that topic. From here, we go to project management topics like incremental development, reuse and project stories.

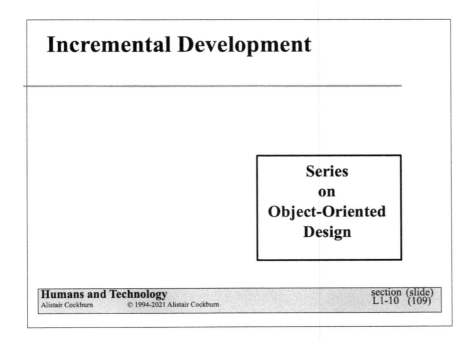

Back in the early 1990s, incremental development was a big topic: "What is the difference between incremental and iterative development?" and "How do you put iterative development on a Gantt chart so it can be scheduled (typically on a fixed-price project)?"

We answered the first question already in 1992. It shows up in my first technical paper on object technology, published in the IBM Systems Journal in 1993 (see: https://web.archive.org/web/20140329210102/http://alistair.cockburn.us/The+impact+of+object+orientation+on+application+development).

I learned how to put incremental development on a linear calendar about that same time, but didn't learn how to put iterative development on a linear calendar until after Project Winifred ended in 1995, where we worked out some rules. The worst to describe was "risk-based" project management, which we didn't even understand back then. I finally learned to describe it bit by bit since 2009 up through now (see https://web.archive.org/web/20140329202950/http://alistair.cockburn.us/Design+as+Knowledge+Acquisition).

It's fun going back and watching my progression in understanding and explaining this. You can follow that learning path here: https://web.archive.org/web/20140329205621/http://alistair.cockburn.us/Pages+about+incremental+and+iterative+development.

Let's see what I knew back in 1994.

Incremental development is piecewise development and integration of the system.

(Do not try to specify it all first, analyze it all, design it all, then test it all.)

Specify as much as comfortable, design and build a piece. Learn from that experience.

Design and build what can be kept in a person's head. Learn from each segment.

With better knowledge, design the next part. Integrate. With better knowledge, ..., ...

(This is OLD news. pre-1980)

Humans and Technology
Alistair Cockburn   © 1994-2021 Alistair Cockburn
section (slide)
L1-10   (110)

Iterative development is learning from experience, and going back to a segment to improve it.

(Do NOT assume you will do your best work first. Estimate where you will come up short.)

Build, incrementally. Test, evaluate, measure. Decide the value of improvement.

Plan to make changes. You will anyway.

Allow 10-20% schedule time for improvements.

(This is more old news. 1980's)

Humans and Technology
Alistair Cockburn   © 1994-2021 Alistair Cockburn
section (slide)
L1-10   (111)

These two definitions are foundational. They really are the key. Incremental is "adding onto", iterative is "revising." The industry lost the distinction once the Rational Unified Process authors mashed everything together. However, we saw projects mixing them up, to disastrous results. As one project executive said, as the light dawned: "Oh, we're iterating when we should be incrementing." Yes.

My OO and agile colleagues at the time hated that I said the word "rework" out loud. But iterative development is exactly rework. That's what it's for. I have no trouble getting project sponsors to pay for the rework when they understand what they're getting for it.

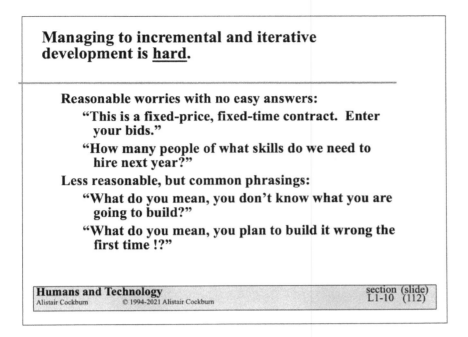

These were the kinds of questions and responses we were getting at the time. Actually, Project Winifred was a fixed-price, fixed-scope project, and we learned how to do iterative as well as incremental development on it. However, we did have to live with some execs making the bottom two comments.

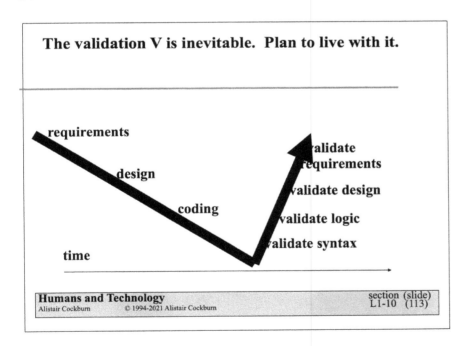

This is how we build out incremental development on a project schedule. Start by recognizing that you can't validate the requirements until you get the design working, which needs the code compiling, which needs the coding done, which needs the design, which needs the requirements. Read this diagram from right to left instead of left to right, and you get a simple fact of life.

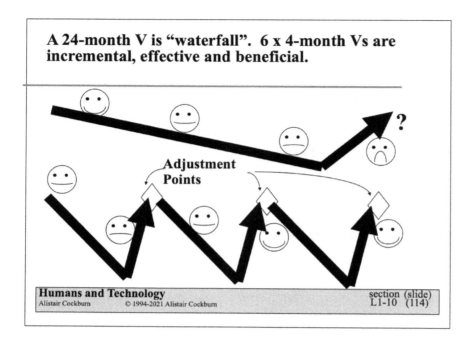

I love making something new out of things people already know. At its worst, incremental development is just a lot of little waterfall projects. And that's not a joke, it really and actually works! In fact, many big companies and governments do big projects in phases: "In phase 1 of this megaproject, we will do A, B, C. In phase 2, we will…" and so on. It is actually standard.

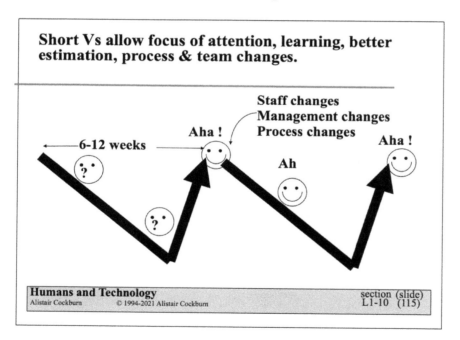

Two things about this graphic. First is the time period: 6-12 weeks. For 1994, that was considered short. But mind you, the project is really delivering to users every 12 weeks, not just giving a demo. The second is the startling number of changes possible at the pause points. This is literally how you go from a failing project to a successful one. We did just that on Project Winifred.

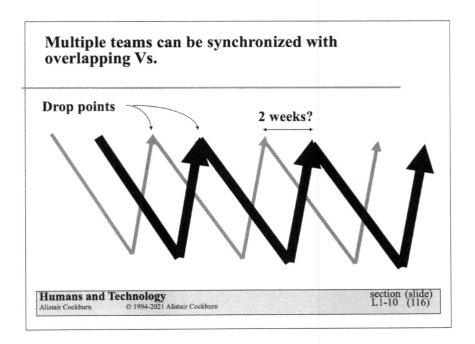

Multiple teams can be synchronized with overlapping Vs.

Drop points

2 weeks?

Humans and Technology
Alistair Cockburn   © 1994-2021 Alistair Cockburn
section (slide)
L1-10   (116)

An advanced topic, one I learned from visiting a team of 150 people writing a new operating system for IBM. They used 2 weeks as the project step timer, synchronizing their work every 2, 4, or 6 weeks.

Objects lend themselves to incremental development.

	□	○	/	AB	❄❄
create	□	□	□	□	□
shift	□	□	□	□	□
alter	□	□	□		□
volume?	□	□			□
stats?	□	□	□	□	

Legend:
☐ v.1.0
☐ v.1.1
☐ v.2
☐ v.3
☐ v.?

Humans and Technology
Alistair Cockburn   © 1994-2021 Alistair Cockburn
section (slide)
L1-10   (117)

The selections of which functions and which objects are selected for each release are not shown. The point is that since objects and verbs are decoupled, the team can literally choose which subset they want for each delivery.

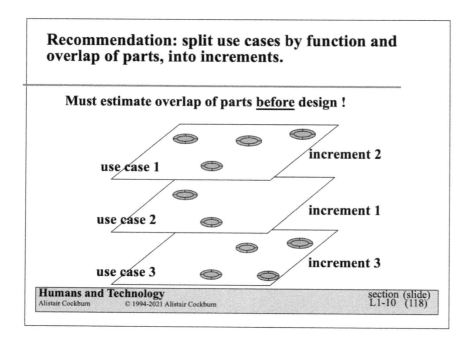

This slide is showing people that they can choose arbitrary parts out of any use cases they like for the first delivery. They are not obliged to deliver all of any one use case at any one time. The business people can select what subsets of the functionality serves them best initially and at each stage.

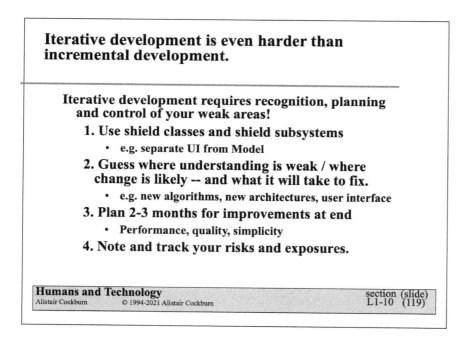

And here my knowledge ended. I had nothing really to say about iterative development. In 2007, I wrote "Three cards for user rights" (
https://web.archive.org/web/20140329205858/http://alistair.cockburn.us/Three+cards+for+user+rights), but that strategy was the one we developed in the 1994-95 Winifred project.

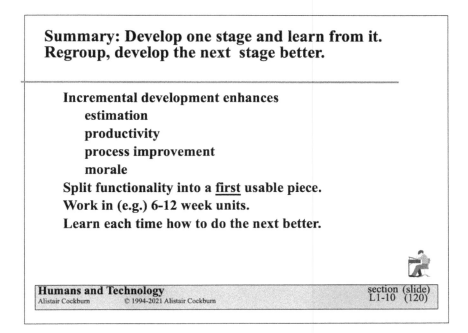

Summary: Develop one stage and learn from it. Regroup, develop the next stage better.

Incremental development enhances
estimation
productivity
process improvement
morale
Split functionality into a <u>first</u> usable piece.
Work in (e.g.) 6-12 week units.
Learn each time how to do the next better.

Humans and Technology
Alistair Cockburn   © 1994-2021 Alistair Cockburn

section (slide)
L1-10 (120)

It is still the case that if I could make one rule for all projects, it would be that all teams deliver running, tested code every 3 months (or sooner). And it is still the case that there are project teams out there that don't do this.

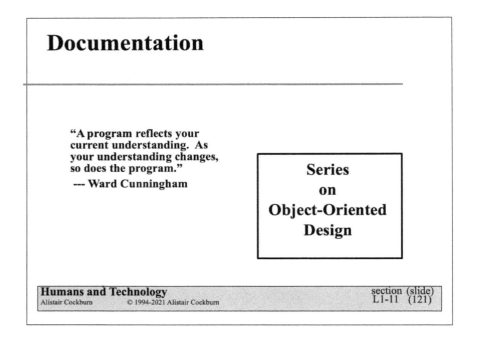

Documentation was always a nasty topic, and doubly so in incremental-iterative projects. There is no right answer. Starting in 1991, researching back to 1968, and continuing forward to now, I have still not found any pat answer that works. You suffer if you write too much, you suffer if you write too little, you suffer if you write the wrong stuff, and no one knows what the right stuff is to write. It is an unpleasant topic all around. And it gets asked every time.

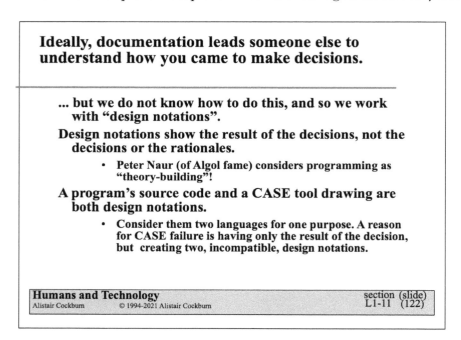

Computer-aided software engineering (CASE) tools were the big thing in the 1990s. Experienced developers didn't like them, because they neither showed the thinking behind the decisions, nor were the delivered code. They were just double labor.

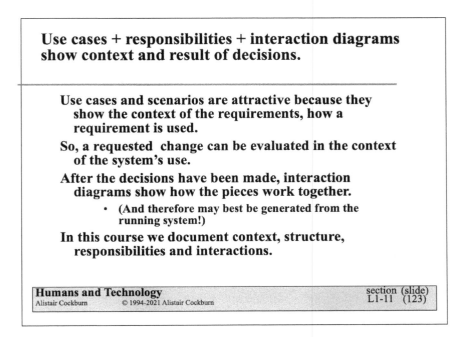

Use cases are better than most formats, because they show the context of use. They don't show the thinking behind decisions. Responsibilities are good for initiating the reader into the intention of a class. They were not supported by most CASE tools, nor written by most programmers.

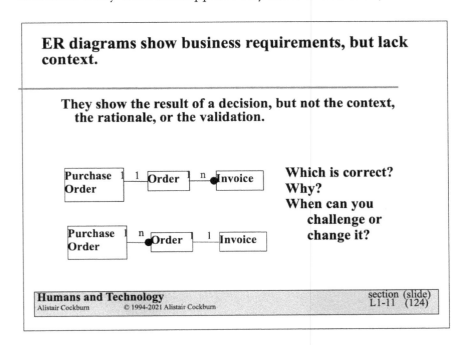

Drawing tools show a structure, but don't answer the question, "Why?"

Open issue: how to capture design rationales, taken decisions, open decisions.

There are too many decisions for each to be written.

Peak rate may be 10 decisions in one minute.

Which ones do you document?

You want to describe:

1. The decisions that have been taken.

2. The decisions or variations still open.

3. What rules any variations must follow.

There is ongoing search for workable ideas:

- MacApp and Taligent frameworks
- Extensible games, design patterns

Humans and Technology
Alistair Cockburn   © 1994-2021 Alistair Cockburn

section (slide)
L1-11 (125)

Many research projects, tool initiatives and pet projects have tried to get designers to capture their design rationales as they go. 25 years later, this still remains a distant goal. Just look at the number of decisions being made per minute: nothing, nothing, nothing, a dozen decisions. How do you capture that on a 50-person, 2-year project?

"Design patterns" are a fresh look at how one might document designs.

Gamma, Helm, Johnson, Vlissides, "Design Patterns"

The design patterns group is taking a new look at how to document designs, trying to address:

1. The context of the requirements.

2. Which decision points were taken.

3. Which variations are compatible.

4. How the current design works.

...these problems show up spectacularly in frameworks!

Humans and Technology
Alistair Cockburn   © 1994-2021 Alistair Cockburn

section (slide)
L1-11 (126)

The *Design Patterns* book had just come out. We thought that would help. It turns out those are design idioms, again saying *what* was decided, but not how the team got to those decisions.

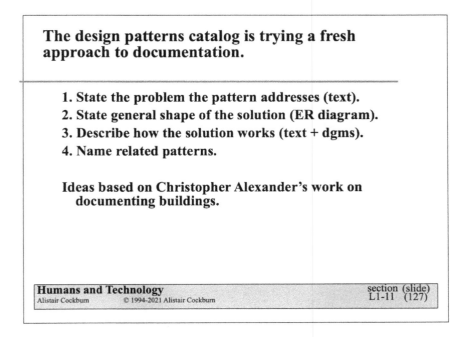

At this point in the course, I was introducing a new crowd to some new and rarified ideas. The point wasn't to get them to truly understand and use them (these were OO newbies, remember?), but to show what was happening at the advanced forefront at the time.

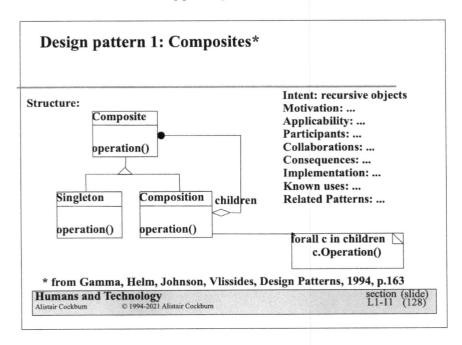

Design pattern 2: Bridge*

Structure:

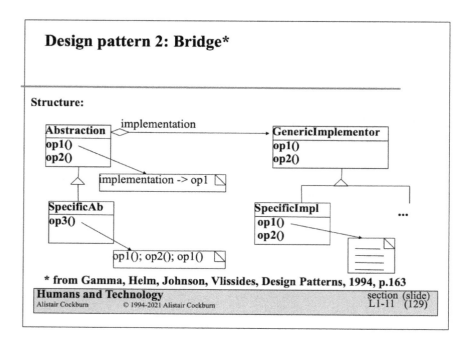

* from Gamma, Helm, Johnson, Vlissides, Design Patterns, 1994, p.163

Humans and Technology
Alistair Cockburn   © 1994-2021 Alistair Cockburn

section (slide)
L1-11 (129)

Summary: Show how the system works in context, plus some reasoning and variations.

1. Use interaction diagrams (text or graphics) to describe the context of operation.

2. Use responsibility statements to succinctly describe the partitioning scheme.

3. Describe (text) reasoning behind non-obvious partitioning decisions.

4. Use ER, FSM, or math in amounts as needed, for business constraints or key ideas.

5. Mark shield objects with the planned variations.

   e.g. computed vs. stored vs. constant values.

Humans and Technology
Alistair Cockburn   © 1994-2021 Alistair Cockburn

section (slide)
L1-11 (130)

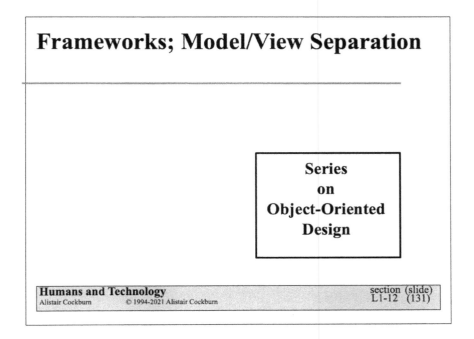

1994 was still the early days of framework design. A few people could do it, and a few people such as Ralph Johnson were exploring how to describe *how* to do it. It was still mystery to me. At the time of this course, I had use frameworks such as Model-View-Controller (MVC), but not designed any myself. I did get to design one myself on our project. Designing it taught me a better way to think and talk when designing with inheritance, so that was useful.

Besides frameworks as a concept, we really wanted everyone on the project to use MVC or one of its simpler variants. So I spent a lot of time on that topic.

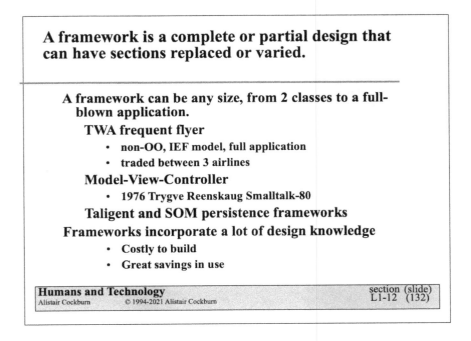

Metaphor: a framework is an alterable game.

1. When completed, it plays a multi-party game.
2. It provides a structure that invokes the pieces.
3. Some rules are fixed, some can be varied.
4. New owner can vary and substitute parts.
5. New owner needs to know:
   - what game it plays
   - what can be varied and what not
   - how the variable areas work together.

Humans and Technology
Alistair Cockburn   © 1994-2021 Alistair Cockburn

section (slide)
L1-12 (133)

Recall that in 1994 we were all exploring ways to talk about using someone else's framework. I can't say this was a great explanation, I certainly wouldn't start that way these days. But okay, it's what I had back then.

Model-View-Controller is a commonly used OO framework.

Problem: Objects' appearances at the UI are changed far more often than their contents.

Cost: Any change to an object may damage it.

Solution: Separate the appearance from the heart. Make 2 or even 3 objects.

How the game plays: The trigger signal hit the controller, who decides whether to wake the model. The view registers itself with the model as interested in changes. When the model changes, it notifies any view registered with it.

Benefits: multiple views, no damage to model.

Humans and Technology
Alistair Cockburn   © 1994-2021 Alistair Cockburn

section (slide)
L1-12 (134)

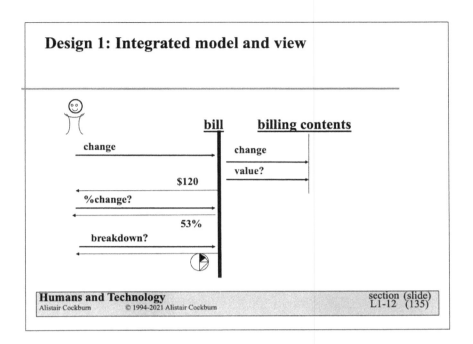

Now we start on the MVC or Model-Interactor (MI) design style. The problem here is that the UI has to encode all the possible questions. For efficiency we may want to partition them:

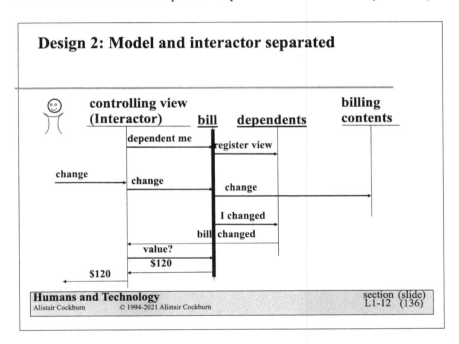

The big deal here is that the Interactor just say's "I'm dependent on you, tell me when you change." The model object just announces, "I changed," and the interactor gets to ask for what it needs.

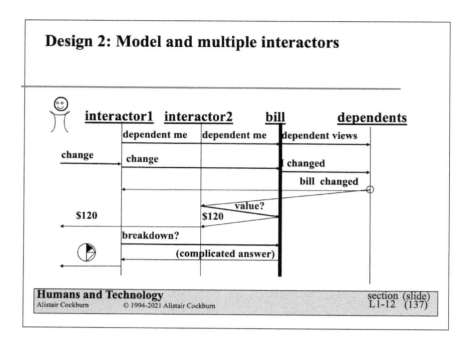

This pays off when two different views care about different things. On a large project, such as a ship, the model is huge. One person might care about structural properties, another about electrical, another about cost, another about furniture. That's too much for one view to know about. Each separate user can get their own interactor that only asks for what they need.

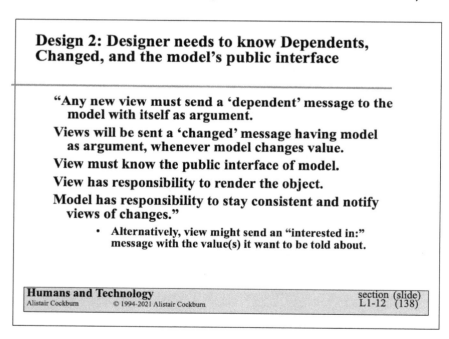

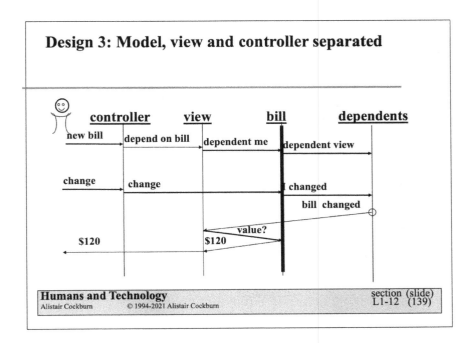

MVC isn't used much anymore, it is a bit complex for most systems. It was invented by Trygve Reenskaug in 1976. He was using an early Smalltalk system to design ships for the Norwegian government, and needed exactly those capabilities. It was a brilliant solution, still the gold standard for design separation for large systems.

In 1998, I arranged a sabbatical year in Norway to go and work with Trygve. Sadly, our project at the Central Bank got into trouble and I didn't have much spare time to learn his new role-modeling technique or his fledgling DCI model. I consider it a privilege to have spent a lot of time with him and his family. He and his wife came and watched my PhD defense in 2003.

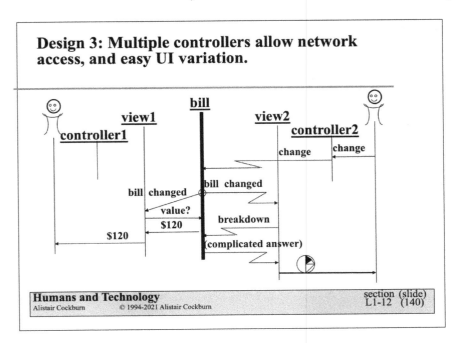

Any frequently solved problem can become a framework.

Persistent data, asset management, transaction histories, user interfaces, network conversation, even a sorted collection.

Only the non-competitive portions of a framework will reach the open market.

Taligent, Template Software, IBM (SOM) are coming to market with libraries of OO frameworks.

Experts suggest the best way to design a framework is to design the same thing several times under different circumstances.

- Only then do the issues become evident.

Humans and Technology
Alistair Cockburn   © 1994-2021 Alistair Cockburn

section (slide)
L1-12 (141)

We take certain kinds of frameworks for granted these days, Ruby on Rails is an example. They become part of the plumbing. Writing a good framework is still an art form.

Summary: Expect frameworks to become standard, but hard to design and understand.

Typically, several designs are done before the tunable areas become apparent.

Documenting frameworks is a difficult art.

Have to discuss design rationales and rules for safe extension.

Expensive to develop, expensive to document, expensive to learn, great saving in use.

A functioning framework saves much because it comes with a prebuilt decision structure.

You, too, can and will design frameworks.

Humans and Technology
Alistair Cockburn   © 1994-2021 Alistair Cockburn

section (slide)
L1-12 (142)

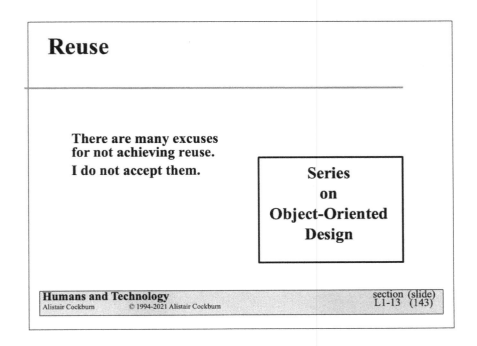

I have to laugh out loud when I read that statement there :)). (yes, that's a double smiley).

Over the years, I have to come to separate three kinds of reuse:
- Find something on the internet and use it.
- Find something that someone else in your company wrote and use it.
- Find something that someone in your team wrote and use it.

Out quest in 1994 was the middle one. That was bad news then and is bad news now. There is too much territorialism within a large company, too much lack of trust of other programmers, and not enough time for the component authors to evolve and maintain their components for other teams.

On the other hand, the first and third are actually quite normal, especially now. People find all sorts of open-source software and use it. They also use function libraries. Within a single team, the trust level is high between colleagues, and they have time to maintain the components.

However, this lecture is almost all a pep talk for the second, plus an accounting of the generally not-discussed costs of searching for components from other places.

P.s., in my 1998 book *Surviving Object-Oriented Projects*, I called it "poly-bloody-hard-reusability", to echo that we cognitively connect the difficulty of a topic with the number of syllables needed to say it. ☺

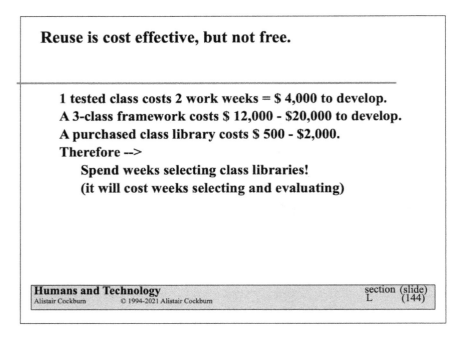

There's the budgeting math. Strange how hard it is to get $1,000 to buy a class library, and how easy it is to spend $4,000 in labor writing the needed parts!

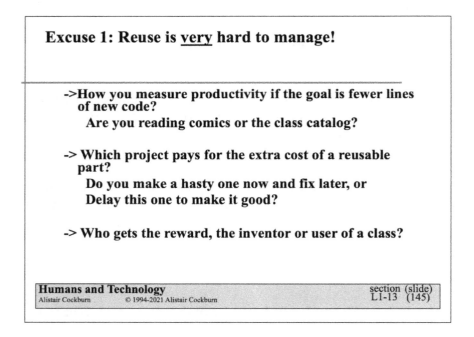

Back then, productivity was often measured in lines of code produced. (It still is, in many places.) That makes if very hard to encourage reuse.

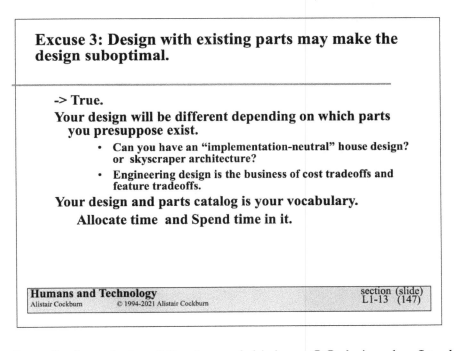

Excuse 2: Reusable parts are hard to find, or poorly documented, tested, and maintained!

->All true.

Corporate reusable parts are available, but typically poorly documented and tested, not maintained.

-> but inexpensive to get, still cost saving.

Industrial reusable parts cost real money, and are showing up on the market.

Humans and Technology
Alistair Cockburn   © 1994-2021 Alistair Cockburn
section (slide)
L   (146)

This is the part about reuse from within the same organization. I don't know that it has ever been solved. A few companies have component-design groups whose sole jobs is to create and maintain components for teams within the organization. It is still a long pull to get that to work.

Excuse 3: Design with existing parts may make the design suboptimal.

-> True.

Your design will be different depending on which parts you presuppose exist.

- Can you have an "implementation-neutral" house design? or skyscraper architecture?
- Engineering design is the business of cost tradeoffs and feature tradeoffs.

Your design and parts catalog is your vocabulary.

Allocate time and Spend time in it.

Humans and Technology
Alistair Cockburn   © 1994-2021 Alistair Cockburn
section (slide)
L1-13 (147)

I was fascinated when I first learned this in an OO design class I took in 1993. We were asked to design a calculator, which we did, with a display controller and all. When our table presented our design, the teacher said, "You know there already is a display controller available?" That component's specs changed our design. When I was a young hardware designer, I was used to designing from catalogs, but had forgotten all about that in the new OO design world!

Excuse 4: People are not mentally, socially trained to spend time seeking, trusting others' code.

-> True again.

Reuse is up to you.

There are too many interesting things to build to waste time rebuilding yet another transaction log or linked list.

Learn to hate redoing existing work.

The topic of reuse is full of empty words.

Just <u>do it</u>.   Yourself.

section (slide)
L1-13 (148)

Yeah, this is the pep talk. Didn't work, of course. Hah.

Reusable parts are "reusable" only after several "reuses"; they are typically thin, not fat.

"Reuse is free. Everything I build is reusable!"
·   -- Senior designer

->What is wrong with that sentence?

"If it has not been reused, it is not reusable."
· Project leader experience report..

A first version usually contains project-specific features that must be taken out.

To make it reusable, remove the project dependencies, making it "thinner".
· do not add "generally useful features", making it fatter.

section (slide)
L1-13 (149)

This might still be new news to some people. Someone says, "I am designing a reusable part." However, what others need and what that person made, they are quite likely to need some changes. Until it gets reused it was never reusable.

Summary: Reuse is costly but cost effective, hard to establish, hard to manage. Allocate time for it.

1. It takes time, energy and money to find and use someone else's software.
2. It takes adjustment on the part of the developer to seek out and use someone else's work.
3. The burden of effort is on the developer, not the manager.
4. Some manager still has to cost justify spending time making a class reusable.
5. All told, there is still a factor of 5:1 or 10:1 in cost savings from reusing parts over developing parts.

Humans and Technology
Alistair Cockburn   © 1994-2021 Alistair Cockburn

section (slide)
L1-13   (150)

This is all still true. I like the sudden reference to managers there :).

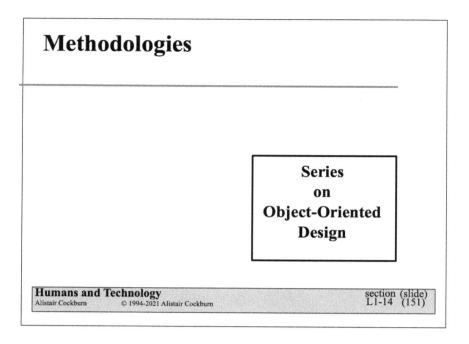

Ahh, methodologies. I ended up getting a Ph.D. in methodologies. "People and Methodologies in Software Development." Actually, it was a Dr. Philos. (Doctor of Philosophy), which is just a tad different. https://www.uio.no/english/research/phd/drphilos/ explains:

Dr. Philos. – another route to a doctoral degree
The Dr. Philos. degree (Doctor Philosophiae) may be awarded to academics who have qualified for a doctoral degree on their own, without formal supervision. Such candidates have no formal affiliation to the University of Oslo until their application for the doctoral examination has been approved.

In other words, I took all my research in methodologies from 1991 to 2002, orchestrated it to meet academic guidelines (with a bit of help from a couple of generous souls), and submitted it as a book in 2003. I write Ph.D. for short sometimes, but those in the know know and care about slight differences. You can read the dissertation here:
https://web.archive.org/web/20140329203845/http://alistair.cockburn.us/People+and+methodologies+in+software+development

In 1994, I didn't know all this. I had studied some projects, and read the popular methodologies of the time. They were all pretty much unsuitable, because they were all tools-centric. We hadn't written the agile manifesto at the time, but I had written the methodology for the IBM Consulting Group by then, and it was all based around being collocated and communicating a lot. No drawing tools, just incremental development, use cases, CRC cards, Design Patterns, and a lot of talking together.

One of the project leads on that project tried to shift away from my methodology to a combination of Booch, Rumbaugh and Shlaer-Mellor, but fortunately the client listening to me instead of him, and our project turned out successfully, as we now understand, due to the lightness of the methodology we used. An early deliberately "agile" success story.

A methodology provides a framework of communication between teams and members.

1: It fosters clear communication.
- 1a. Allow another person to understand previous work.
- 1a. States deliverables and standards for them.
- Interpersonal responsibilities. Team processes.

2: It forms a basis for education.
- 2a. Guidance on use of techniques.

3: It is larger than 1 person.
- 3a. 1 person needs a technique, 10 people need a methodology.
- 3b. The job description is part of the methodology

-Hiring a person to do a job is a fact of the methodology.

Humans and Technology
Alistair Cockburn   © 1994-2021 Alistair Cockburn

section (slide)
L1-14 (152)

If "reuse" appears too easy because it only has two syllables, then "methodology" appears too hard because it has five syllables. A methodology is really only the conventions a team adopts. That is pretty easy. However, I didn't know that at the time. This slide says what I did know at the time, and is still all correct. I love the phrase my tech-mentor Dick Antalek gave me: "Hiring a person to do a job is a fact of the methodology."

Most OO published "methodologies" provide insufficient guidance, are overly cumbersome.

Most (Booch, Rumbaugh, Shlaer&Mellor, Odell) focus on design notation: a standard/ a deliverable/ a technique

Most have insufficient tool support.

   Change the code, then go change the design sheet.

Most have a process that says, "Try. Iterate".

Role statements, technique guides, deliverables guides, standards, process guides, tool guides are missing.

Each has some attractions and some drawbacks.

Learn how to appreciate their qualities.
- BUT, Do NOT feel compelled to merge them!

Humans and Technology
Alistair Cockburn   © 1994-2021 Alistair Cockburn

section (slide)
L1-14 (153)

The key phrase here is that you can't add methodologies together. The result is too heavy.

Booch attractions: rich notation, famous author , corporate backing.

o The first "object" "methodology" published.

o Sold over 100,000 copies.

o Booch committed to absorbing all notations

  Down to C++ coding level (parallel syntax?)

  Logical, physical, structural, behavioral diagramming.

o Backed by Rational Corp, with courses and tools

  Evolving capabilities.

o 1994: Booch teaming with Rumbaugh to unify ideas.

Humans and Technology
Alistair Cockburn   © 1994-2021 Alistair Cockburn

section (slide)
L1-14 (154)

Booch drawbacks: too rich a notation, hard to maintain, changing fast.

o Day 1: subset the notation

  No project can use and remember it all.

o After day 1: devise a process

  It contains no process guide

o Install a change control process

  Changing code invalidates the design model.

  Rational working on reverse engineering tools.

o Be prepared to evolve

  Booch steadily learning, absorbing, changing.

Humans and Technology
Alistair Cockburn   © 1994-2021 Alistair Cockburn

section (slide)
L1-14 (155)

The common theme in all the "methodologies" described here is that they were basically all just drawing notations. In the sense of "job descriptions" they came up rather empty. In other words, we would have to make up our own process, anyway.

OMT attractions: rich notation, compatible with pre-OO practices, gives design guidance.

o Structural and behavioral modeling notations.

o ER, data-flow and FSM diagrams
   People familiar with them.

o Specific chapters in book on finding and evaluating classes, database design, etc.

o 1994: Rumbaugh teaming with Booch to unify ideas.

Humans and Technology
Alistair Cockburn   © 1994-2021 Alistair Cockburn

section (slide)
L1-14 (156)

OMT drawbacks: too many notations, hard to maintain, changing and out-of-date.

o Everything but the kitchen sink; Don't try to use it all.

o Academic; Hard for standard practitioners.
   And getting more academic over time.

o Process: Different projects need different setups.

o Inadequate tools to manage changes in code.

o Be prepared to evolve.
   Rumbaugh steadily evolving.
   Change with him as he learns more and better.

Humans and Technology
Alistair Cockburn   © 1994-2021 Alistair Cockburn

section (slide)
L1-14 (157)

The common theme I got out of all my project interviews from 1991-1994 (and in fact, since then) was that the diagrams were a duplicate description of what the code said. That meant that as the code changed, the programmer would have to go back and update the drawings by hand. That would never be done correctly, so the drawings were guaranteed to get out of date quite quickly.

Objectory attractions: use cases, metamodel, relatively complete, traceable products.

o First OO methodologist with functional
requirements and formal interaction diagrams.
o Covers requirements gathering through test.
o Methodology includes process, even models itself!
Tuneable development process
o Traceability and code generation built into tools.
o Jacobson has 30 years of experience in telecomm.

Humans and Technology
Alistair Cockburn   © 1994-2021 Alistair Cockburn

section (slide)
L1-14   (158)

Objectory drawbacks: cumbersome in practice, missing design guidance.

o Usage reports indicate very heavy process
Constraining, cumbersome deliverables
"Must be good for large projects"
o Focus on deliverables, short on techniques
Recently adopted responsibility-based design
o Short experience with application development
Developed from telecommunications background
o "Use cases" overused, unclear in the industry.
Lovely buzzword, conflicting definitions

Humans and Technology
Alistair Cockburn   © 1994-2021 Alistair Cockburn

section (slide)
L1-14   (159)

Booch and co. at Rational bought Ivar Jacobson's company Objectory. (Remember Ivar Jacobson, creator of use cases? Yes, him.). Then they bought/merged with Rumbaugh, and merged all their ideas and produced the Rational Unified Process. But that hadn't happened yet.

Objectory did have roles and techniques and was tailorable. However, I had done some research on it, and found it to be very heavy, much more than what any normal project would need.

Ptech attractions: compatible with pre-OO practices, formal, clean & readable notation.

o "Objectified" structured analysis notation.
　　ER diagrams with inheritance
　　Data-flow diagrams with no data stores
　　Event modeling with event subclassing
o Sophisticated and precise semantics
　　Possible to generate code and execute directly
o Simple enough for users to read and even write
　　Demonstrated
o Complete notation, even object reclassification.

Humans and Technology
Alistair Cockburn　　　© 1994-2021 Alistair Cockburn

section (slide)
L1-14　(160)

Ptech drawbacks: no provision for reuse, hard to translate to design.

o Techniques focus on fresh development each time.
　　No discussion of "design with reuse"
　　No place for "design patterns"
o Fully separate function and object models
　　Hard to find where the class boundaries belong.

Humans and Technology
Alistair Cockburn　　　© 1994-2021 Alistair Cockburn

section (slide)
L1-14　(161)

I was being thorough. You are unlikely to have heard of Ptech. It was sophisticated, but by now you know the story: Keep It Simple. Collaborate – Deliver – Reflect – Improve. Drop the ceremony as low as you can. Focus on communication.

Coad attractions: simple, complete notation.

o **Single notation encompasses object interaction diagrams and ER diagrams.**

 In advance of its time. May become more popular.

o **Simple process: analyze a bit, design a bit, build a bit.**

Humans and Technology
Alistair Cockburn   © 1994-2021 Alistair Cockburn

section (slide)
L1-14 (162)

Coad drawbacks: simplistic, lacks supporting tools, bad design guidance.

o **Simple drawing notation requires sophisticated tools to be effective**

 Not available yet, but check around 2002.

o **Books contain naive or questionable advice**

 E.g. employee subclass of person

o **Wouldn't it be nice if developing OO systems were so easy!!**

 Missing attention to algorithms.

o **Still missing interteam processes.**

Humans and Technology
Alistair Cockburn   © 1994-2021 Alistair Cockburn

section (slide)
L1-14 (163)

I don't really have to say too much about this.

Shlaer/Mellor attractions: formal, event-driven, metamodel, compatible with pre-OO CASE tools.

o **Design ideas based on their experience in event-driven, real-time systems.**

  Handles asynchronous, real-time demands

o **Complete deliverables from analysis down to code.**

o **Established market with non-OO CASE tools**

  Save money - reuse the CASE tool

o **Good discussion of object life cycles.**

Humans and Technology
Alistair Cockburn   © 1994-2021 Alistair Cockburn

section (slide)
L1-14 (164)

Shlaer/Mellor drawbacks: improper CASE tool support, hard to maintain, too much analysis.

o **Inadequate tools - must reenter information by hand.**

  Time consuming and frustrating

o **Change in lower-level design forces rework in higher design**

  Fixable with better tools?

o **Excessive time in paper analysis and paper design**

  **Coding is easy from the final design document   --
  if your project lives that long**

Humans and Technology
Alistair Cockburn   © 1994-2021 Alistair Cockburn

section (slide)
L1-14 (165)

Interestingly, Steven Mellor was invited to the meeting of the agile manifesto and became one of the manifesto authors. We all stared at him, like, What is He Doing Here? He famously introduced himself with, "I'm Steven Mellor, and I'm a spy."

In the end, we found that for all our seeming differences, we were operating from the same value center, and got along without friction during the writing of the manifesto. I am fairly sure that his presence kept us from getting too excited and one-side during the manifesto writing, which just goes to show you.

Wirfs-Brock attractions: effective, simple, good design guidance.

o **Responsibilities demonstrated effective on multiple projects.**

    Consistently highly rated by busy designers

    Valid for subsystem as well as class design

o **Easy to state, relatively easy to learn.**

o **Book provides thorough discussion of design issues.**

Humans and Technology
Alistair Cockburn   © 1994-2021 Alistair Cockburn   section (slide) L1-14 (166)

Wirfs-Brock drawbacks: design technique only, no use cases or interaction diagrams

o No requirements, coding or test included.

    "Designing OO Software" is an accurate title

o Needs addition of use cases for requirements, interaction diagrams for documentation.

    (She is using those now)

o Good technique, needs to be complemented with other techniques and processes.

Humans and Technology
Alistair Cockburn   © 1994-2021 Alistair Cockburn   section (slide) L1-14 (167)

As you know, we adopted this, but as a central technique to use, not a full methodology for our team. Still love it to this day, still my central design technique.

This course attractions: effective, simple, has a metamodel, design guidance, relatively complete.

o Second generation methodology, based on project debriefings from previous methodologies.

o Responsibilities as cornerstone, from Wirfs-Brock.

o Use cases as cornerstone, from Jacobson.

o Design technique gleaned from expert designers.

 Includes "design with reuse" and "design patterns".

o Metamodel ensured completeness and tool guidance.

o Implicit roles and processes.

Humans and Technology
Alistair Cockburn   © 1994-2021 Alistair Cockburn

section (slide)
L1-14 (168)

This course drawbacks: no deliverables description, no process guidelines, no tool support.

o Still incomplete against the methodology framework:

 Multiple processes possible

 No business rule modeling

 No document standards.

o No tool vendors with full support of: use cases, responsibilities, class design.

 Check again in mid 1996.

 These three likely to become the staple of Booch and Rumbaugh and Jacobson over time.

Humans and Technology
Alistair Cockburn   © 1994-2021 Alistair Cockburn

section (slide)
L1-14 (169)

This course was taught to our full project team in 1994. What we already knew about use case and responsibility-based design was correct at the beginning and didn't change, although I definitely learned about how to connect and view 240 use cases! We learned more about iterative development over the 18 months of the project. We learned about cross-functional teams, the value of colocation, testing and many other details. But the heart of the project success came from the selected elements of the methodology plus heavy, heavy emphasis on just plain old communication and common sense.

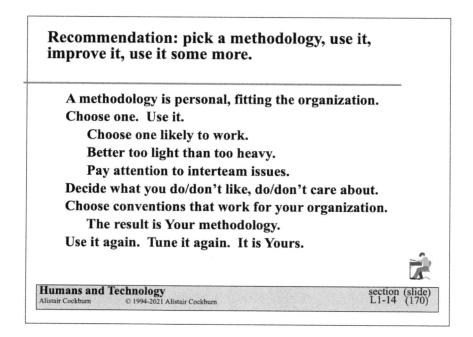

This slide is actually more interesting that it might appear at first glance.

First, it says to update the methodology periodically. That is core result in my Dr. Philos. thesis and in all my work since 1994. Not just a team retrospective, but really questioning the "conventions the team agrees to follow" every few months or as staff changes. "Use it again. Tune it again."

"Better too light than too heavy" is a great phrase. A methodology should be made too small to start with, and added onto only where it comes up short. The reverse, starting with a bigger one and trying to make it lighter, doesn't work.

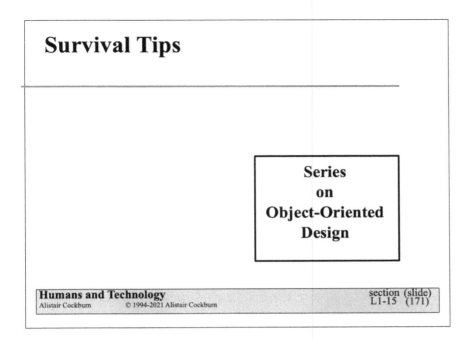

Sort of a top-ten list, things that I had learned from my project interviews, 1991-94.

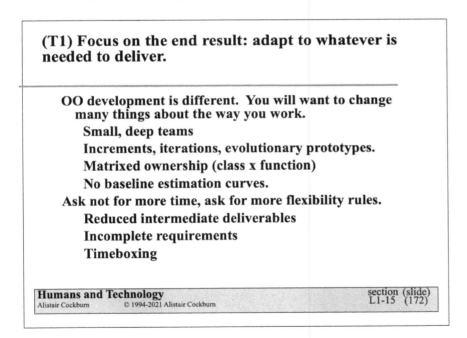

Yeah, all of those were difficult topics in the 1990s. Oddly, the clients on the Winifred project already had most of those in place. They already had done user-centric, incremental, collocated development. Our trouble was more with the IBM managers. It's not actually that "OO development" was different, it's that we were doing agile development, with a new technology.

(T2) Control expectations: OO is just a packaging technology that lets us think differently.

Otherwise rational people suddenly believe they can do 10x as much in 1/10 the time.

You can do more in less
* with lot of practice
* and a good reuse library

OO does not generate any code for you... it lets you reuse code artfully.

OO does not make (business model) = (code model)
* Good subclassing is an art, born of thinking, experience, luck and revision.

Humans and Technology
Alistair Cockburn   © 1994-2021 Alistair Cockburn

section (slide)
L1-15 (173)

People used think object technology would make then 10x more productive. (Hmm, sounds like certain agile sales pitches, doesn't it?)

(T3) Get useful tools: #1-versioning, #2-lan work, #3-hyperlinks, ... beware partial code generation.

Versioning: the most difficult thing to do manually.
    Do it, however is needed, for everything.

Lan working eases sharing of results.
    Check-in, check-out

Hyperlinks: still mostly a wish, but making progress
    Get from any keyword to code, model, or glossary

Partial code generation does not survive iterations.

"CASE" tools: drawing editors, but expensive.
    (and do not survive iterations.)

Humans and Technology
Alistair Cockburn   © 1994-2021 Alistair Cockburn

section (slide)
L1-15 (174)

Versioning is now mostly taken care of, most project teams use Git. LAN was early/pre-internet, that's all ok now. Project glossaries still aren't a thing, nor is hyperlinking from requirements or documentation to models and code, even though hyperlinking is almost everywhere. And as I wrote earlier, CASE tools didn't allow you to maintain the code in the tool, so they caused double maintenance. Some people just used a simple drawing tool to the same effect.

Expertise: hire some or rent some, but get some.

There are so many great pitfalls, you don't need to fall
into the same old ones.

There is so much to learn.

Try "just-in-time" education

Find experts:

OO project manager

OO team communicator (methodology)

Language specialist

Class library specialist

Humans and Technology
Alistair Cockburn   © 1994-2021 Alistair Cockburn

section (slide)
L1-15 (175)

I ended up being one of those hired expert types :). Companies are more used to hiring coaches
these days. However, there is less to learn now, the entire internet culture and migration to
digital organizations, the remote work during the pandemic, all have changed culture so much.
In 1994, this was all so new, and no specific pressure to oblige people to learn.

**(T5) Use cases + algorithms + responsibilities:
necessary and sufficient (but not optimal)**

Designers and methodologists are converging on use cases
for requirements, responsibilities for partitioning.

Opinions are split on use of class diagrams.

* Some favor complete modeling

* Some favor occasional use

No methodology discusses algorithms.

Algorithms are personal, methodology is for teams.

Humans and Technology
Alistair Cockburn   © 1994-2021 Alistair Cockburn

section (slide)
L1-15 (176)

There was no way to discuss this ultralight, communication-centric way of working seven years
before the agile manifesto. Look at me struggling here. Now we just say "agile." Haha ☺

(T6) Achieve reuse: it depends on YOU trusting your predecessors!

10-20 work-days to invent, test and document a class.

.5-1 work-days to learn to use one.

    Is your ego worth loss of x20 in productivity?

Do you really want to spend your life coding linked lists?

Reuse is hard to manage:

    Who is goofing off, who is learning the library?

    How does one brag about writing 10 loc/day?

    How does one measure productivity?

    Reward the creator or the user of a class?

Reuse is up to you. Do it.

Humans and Technology
Alistair Cockburn   © 1994-2021 Alistair Cockburn

section (slide)
L1-15 (177)

I have to laugh a bit at the hard sell on reuse. It did no good, of course. Open-source software has increased reuse so much: As one person said, "When reuse is working right, you just say 'use'. You don't "reuse" a hammer, you just use it." Thus it is with open-source: you just use those frameworks and libraries. That's true reuse. Reusable components within a company is still hard.

(T7) Manage your use of C++: find the key 60% and stick to it.

Moving to C++ has nearly sunk two companies and has drowned many projects.

It is a large language with many alternatives.

    Ignore 40% and use the key 60%.

    (Object message... Object message...Object message)

Problem 1: which 60% is the correct set to use?

Problem 2: How do you get everyone to use that 60%?

Get a C++ expert (a real one) to help you select the 60% for your organization.

It is up to you to stay with that 60%.

Humans and Technology
Alistair Cockburn   © 1994-2021 Alistair Cockburn

section (slide)
L1-15 (178)

In my 1998 *Surviving Object-Oriented Projects* book, I wrote that the use of C++ in IT projects was one of the top predictors of project failure. :)). (yes, there's that double laugh again). In this course, I couldn't say that, so I wrote the safest advice I could conjure up.

(T8) Design with shield classes: know where you are putting flexibility.

Shields are conscious design choices.
... have a match in the domain, ideally.
... protect a set of subclasses.
... package an interface with multiple variations.
... should be both obvious, and documented, at the end.

Humans and Technology
Alistair Cockburn   © 1994-2021 Alistair Cockburn
section (slide)
L1-15 (179)

This was a topic for the advanced designer-programmers to watch over. It was too subtle for beginners.

(T9) Develop incrementally: it eases mid-course adjustments.

People learn by doing to completion.
Do one increment in 4-8 weeks.
Take time to examine & adjust after every increment:
    way of work, teams, process, estimates, education, ...
Use the validation V to your advantage.

Humans and Technology
Alistair Cockburn   © 1994-2021 Alistair Cockburn
section (slide)
L1-15 (180)

This is a good slide. Most teams know this by now (27 years later!). You know this, or you wouldn't be reading this book. There are, however, still teams that fight every sentence on this slide.

(T10) Plan time to rework: you will rework anyway.

Iteration is harder on a manager than are increments.
  It means doing something twice.
Identify and separate sections likely to change.
Plan a 2-month period to clean up and improve key areas.
  Programs rewritten a second time are shorter, faster,
    <u>and</u> easier to maintain.
  Better for your experienced team to do it with fresh
    memories, than for your maintenance team to do it
    without understanding.

Humans and Technology
Alistair Cockburn   © 1994-2021 Alistair Cockburn

section (slide)
L1-15 (181)

Rework was a dirty word in 1994, it still is, even in agile circles. Although, I think it is an odd piece of advice that bit about "plan a 2-month period to clean up and improve." That's what I had been told in my early project interviews. I don't think I've seen that more than just a few times in about 30 years of watching projects, though. And "write it second time": don't think I've ever seen in person.

(T11) Train your manager: increments and the difference between activity and progress.

Managers have to fix time and budget,
  and have to plan iterations within that.
They cannot support YOU if they do not understand
  what you are doing.
  Are you getting great reuse or reading books?
  Writing new code or cutting and pasting?

Final test: what is wrong with this statement?
  • "C++ is really productive - I can write 500 loc/day"

Humans and Technology
Alistair Cockburn   © 1994-2021 Alistair Cockburn

section (slide)
L1-15 (182)

Delivering every increment supports your manager as well as your team. But these days, managers should understand incremental development. P.s. that last question I leave as homework for the interested reader. :)

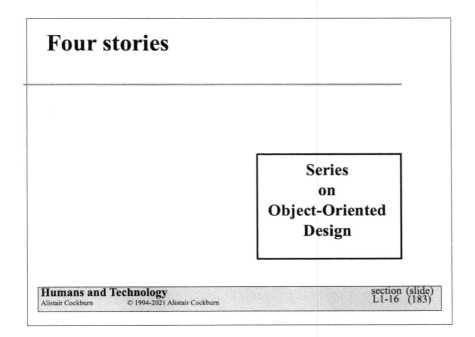

I was known for collecting stories, even back then. In fact, on project Winifred I lived off the stories I had gathered. "I heard a story from another team," I'd say. "In this situation they did the following…," and then I'd tell what they did. We'd think about it and do that. It worked, every time. Eventually, I stopped telling the story and just said the what-to-do part. That's when I really became a consultant (where's the crying laughing emoticon?)

I used the following four stories to anchor a set of recommendations before the project. They also (along with project Winifred) ended up in *Surviving Object-Oriented Projects*.

Story 1: The case of too much prototyping.

Beginning: no OO background, no OO education
"OO is prototyping - we'll prototype until we like the product, then convert it to product code."
--medium sized Smalltalk project
Middle:
Audience: "This prototype is too slow!
Audience: "This prototype is too slow!"
Executive: "You don't take feedback. Turn this prototype into a product now, or get cut."
End: cut.

Humans and Technology
Alistair Cockburn   © 1994-2021 Alistair Cockburn
section (slide)
L1-16 (184)

Lessons from the case of too much prototyping: use a Requirements Model, dispose of it quickly.

"Rapid Prototypes" do not evolve into code, but expectations say they do.
Create a Requirements Model, but make sure either:
   (a) it is product quality and can turn into product,
   (b) or it vanishes as soon as possible.
Diminishing Visible Returns in back half of project is hard to manage.
   Work in increments to control Diminishing Visible Returns.

Humans and Technology
Alistair Cockburn   © 1994-2021 Alistair Cockburn
section (slide)
L1-16 (185)

This was my first ever interview! These people were user-centric, iterative designers (read: "agile", back in 1991!). They made a kiosk and put it in the hall. Everyone complained about the speed. They said, "Don't worry about the speed, tell us about the usage." The people said, "It's just too slow." They repeated that until management said, "Make it fast enough to stop the complaining." They couldn't (Smalltalk used to be *really* slow), and the project was canceled.

My main lesson was: If you are going to prototype, prototype in a language you can't possibly ship in, so they can't make you ship it. The B.U.G. project did exactly that., see the next story.

Story 2: The case of Brooklyn Union Gas

Beginning: Consultants, but not deep OO ones.
　　Bet-your-company, main line project
　　150 mainframe programmers
　　"We'll write our own PL/1 variant to do OO"
　　Large, mainframe, non-GUI, relational database.
Middle:
　　??　<-- "What did they do?!"
End:
　　Successfully delivered and working
　　Produced and being maintained.

Humans and Technology	section (slide)
Alistair Cockburn　　　© 1994-2021 Alistair Cockburn	L1-16　(186)

Lessons from the B.U.G. case: Plan for danger, set and follow simple standards, be conservative.

Technology was considered new, likely to change. So:
　　1. Reduced use of inheritance because it is hard to change on disk.
　　2. Iterations in key areas, e.g., run time.
　　3. Simple standards followed consistently
Use cases and responsibilities (or things like them) work. Graphical notation is unnecessary or worse.
OO can be done on any platform, in any language.

Humans and Technology	section (slide)
Alistair Cockburn　　　© 1994-2021 Alistair Cockburn	L1-16　(187)

This the case of when people do everything right, you can't see what they did. I was just starting out, knew nothing, spent a day interviewing them, and learned basically nothing. Hence the "???" in the middle part. I did learn that it is useful to heavily subset the methodology and have some simple standards, also a note about prototyping, but I couldn't understand the magic.

About prototyping: The project lead prototyped the system in LISP (yes, he was that good), so they had a reference implementation to lean on. And since they obviously couldn't make their main billing system out of his prototype, they put 150 people on the project for two years. The lesson of only prototype in a technology you can't possibly ship in.

Story 3: the case of following a recipe.

Beginning: no OO background, self-taught
  "Just model the world and turn into objects."
  large, multinational, PC / host
Middle:
  PC people in one department, host in another
    - no cooperation
  "Naive" real-world model, failed 1st deliverable.
  Converting to objects did not help.
End: Struggling to convert and save project.

Humans and Technology	section (slide)
Alistair Cockburn © 1994-2021 Alistair Cockburn	L1-16 (188)

Lessons from the case of following a recipe: keep your eyes open, communicate well.

Host/WS teams is necessary but dangerous. Create owners for functions and classes.
  - Matrix model of ownership
Do not trust to a recipe, have to always be thinking.
  Do not "just" model the world.
  Only in hindsight does the design model the world.
"OO is not programming as usual"

Humans and Technology	section (slide)
Alistair Cockburn © 1994-2021 Alistair Cockburn	L1-16 (189)

There was myth in the early days that object technology just meant "model the world and program it up." I discussed that already on slide 1, and again on slide 41. There are many valid models of the business, but very few also make good programs, meeting performance and other resource goals.

Also here we see the failure of splitting teams by the technology section they own. I had already worked out the matrix model by then, which we eventually got to try on project Winifred.

Story 4: the case of the agile project.

Beginning: no OO expertise
   large, C++ development, 2 work groups
   Got permission to use increments, even on the
      requirements and schedule creation.
Middle:
   Crashed 1st iteration. Replaced programmers. Got
      3 months education. Tied managers together.
   Tardy 2nd iteration. Matrix model. Everyone codes.
   Timely 3rd iteration. Tuned structure and process.
End: on time, expanded to muli-site interleaved project.

Humans and Technology
Alistair Cockburn   © 1994-2021 Alistair Cockburn

section (slide)
L1-16 (190)

Lessons from the case of the agile project: ask for flexibility, keep your eye on the deliverables.

**Focus on the end result, and adjust as you have to to
   get there.**
Matrix model of functions x classes works.
**Use incremental development to provide places to
   replace, fix, tune your operation.**
Don't ask for more time, ask for more flexibility.

Humans and Technology
Alistair Cockburn   © 1994-2021 Alistair Cockburn

section (slide)
L1-16 (191)

Okay, this is weird. I did not touch these slides, I promise. I found them in an archived folder and am publishing them as is. Literally until this moment, writing the words for this slide, I had no recollection of ever having used the word 'agile'. Blows me away. In *Surviving Object-Oriented Projects*, I call it project Ingrid. The word 'agile' doesn't even show up in the index. So cool.

This project interview was foundational for me. They ran quarterly increments, failed after the first. But then they held their first "interim retrospective" (they didn't have a word for it), and changed *everything* about the project, the teams, the management, everything. I had never seen or heard of such a thing before. This project became my model for running projects after that.

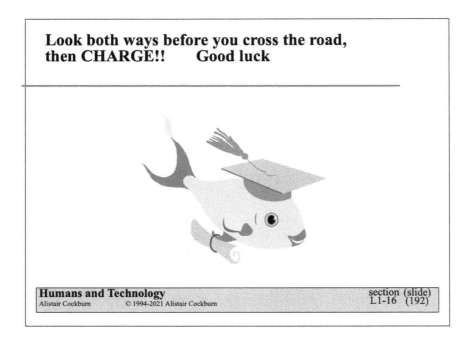

That is the end of the course. Now you know everything that the students in that class knew. :) Except you also have the benefit of twenty years of agile culture, hexagonal architecture better articulated, and so on.

I hope you enjoyed that tour of the old course. I hope that if you previously did not know about responsibility-driven design, or anything else that was mentioned, you will look them up. Everything should still be available to read. Most of the people mentioned are still alive.

What follows are a handful of selected "reminder" slides taken from the course deck so that students wouldn't have to go back through 190 slides to find the key points, and the exercises we used in the course.

For the future, we just learned that I have permission from Pearson Education to make an audiobook of *Surviving Object-Oriented Projects* and the original *Agile Software Development*. I hope to not just read them out loud (myself, of course), but also make them *annotated* versions, as this course is, with notes about what I've learned since then, or on background stories. In addition, I may be able to rehydrate my instructional writings on *Using CRC Cards* and *Responsibility-Based Modeling*. As an addendum to this course, I might write out the answers to the exercised used in this course. Let's hope, and see if all of those come out sometime soon.

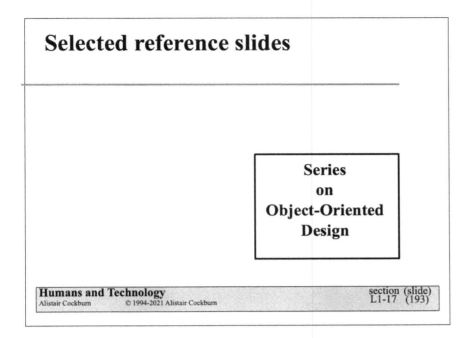

Selected reference slides

Series
on
Object-Oriented
Design

Humans and Technology
Alistair Cockburn   © 1994-2021 Alistair Cockburn

section (slide)
L1-17 (193)

I won't comment on these slides, all the commentary was already given the first time. They are here for quick reference.

A methodology provides a framework of communication between teams and members.

1: It fosters clear communication.
- 1a. Allow another person to understand previous work.
- 1a. States deliverables and standards for them.
- Interpersonal responsibilities. Team processes.

2: It forms a basis for education.
- 2a. Guidance on use of techniques.

3: It is larger than 1 person.
- 3a. 1 person needs a technique, 10 people need a methodology.
- 3b. The job description is part of the methodology

-Hiring a person to do a job is a fact of the methodology.

Humans and Technology
Alistair Cockburn   © 1994-2021 Alistair Cockburn

section (slide)
L1-14 (194)

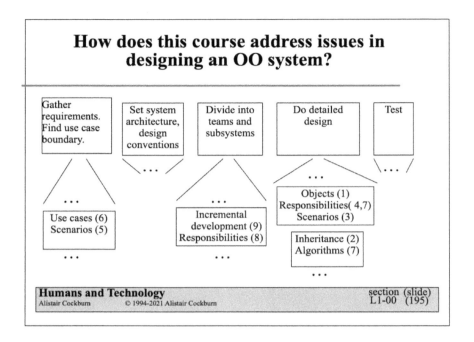

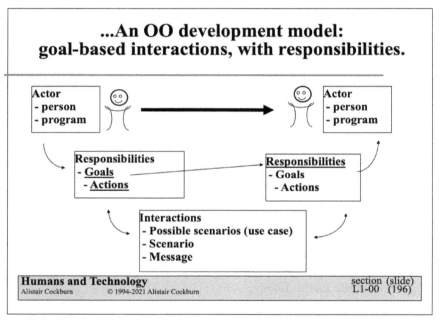

Recommendation: split use cases by function and overlap of parts, into increments.

Must estimate overlap of parts <u>before</u> design !

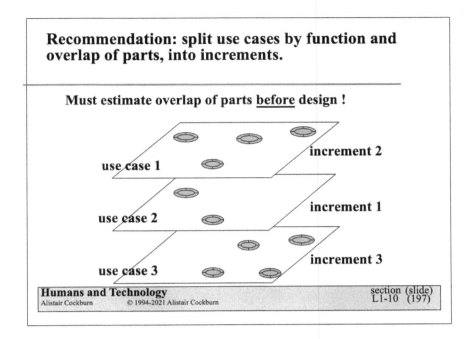

Short Vs allow focus of attention, learning, better estimation, process & team changes.

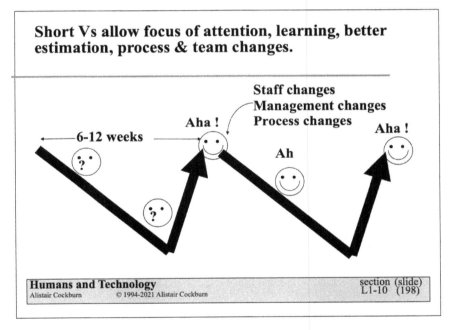

A use case has success and failure outcomes, a scenario has only one outcome.

Primary Actor: Account owner Primary Actor's Goal: withdraw money			Use case characteristic information
Knows codes, Has funds.	Knows codes, No funds here, Other funds.	Knows codes, Not sufficient funds anywhere	Scenario conditions
Presses button.	Presses button.	Presses button.	Trigger
Get codes. ok. Ask amount.ok. Give money.	Get codes. ok. Ask amount.Nok. Transfer funds ok. Give money	Get codes. ok. Ask amount. Nok. Transfer funds. Fail. Refuse money.	Scenario steps
Succeed		Failure	Outcome

Humans and Technology
Alistair Cockburn   © 1994-2021 Alistair Cockburn

section (slide)
L1-07 (199)

Use cases contain scenarios, which reference use cases, which use scenarios, etc. - continually smaller.

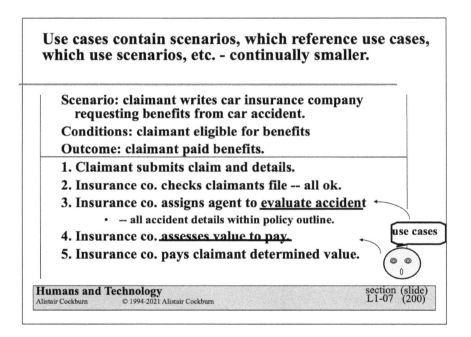

Scenario: claimant writes car insurance company requesting benefits from car accident.

Conditions: claimant eligible for benefits

Outcome: claimant paid benefits.

1. Claimant submits claim and details.
2. Insurance co. checks claimants file -- all ok.
3. Insurance co. assigns agent to evaluate accident
   - -- all accident details within policy outline.
4. Insurance co. assesses value to pay.
5. Insurance co. pays claimant determined value.

use cases

Humans and Technology
Alistair Cockburn   © 1994-2021 Alistair Cockburn

section (slide)
L1-07 (200)

Summarize functional requirements in 4-columns: actor, goal, system responsibility, data needs.

ATM actor	goal	system responsibility	data needs
account owner	withdraw money	give $, receipt; update balance	acct #, code, amount.
bank employee	refill cash drawer	update cash balance.	$ amount.
maintenance staff	refill paper	register paper (non)empty	paper present.
tester	test many situations	read/run test scripts, & produce report.	test scripts.
installer	initialize system	reset to start state.	"initialize" signal.

Humans and Technology
Alistair Cockburn   © 1994-2021 Alistair Cockburn   section (slide) L1-06 (201)

Summarize interface requirements in a table: use case, trigger, secondary actors, interface types.

use case	trigger	secondary actors	interface type
withdraw money	key press	bank central cash dispenser	database table. hot link.
refill cash drawer	lift $ sensor	cash dispenser	hot link
test many situations	program command	server computer	flat file.
initialize system	key press	none	- - -

Humans and Technology
Alistair Cockburn   © 1994-2021 Alistair Cockburn   section (slide) L1-07 (202)

Use cases and scenarios provide the material for responsibility-based partitioning.

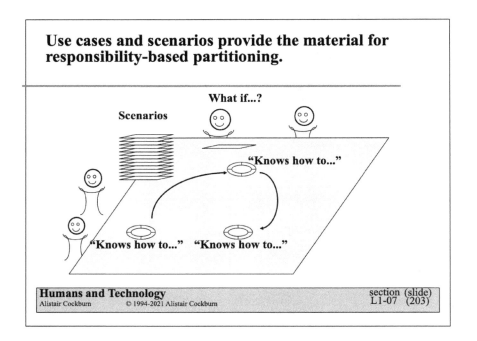

Humans and Technology
Alistair Cockburn   © 1994-2021 Alistair Cockburn

section (slide)
L1-07 (203)

The statement of responsibilities is the shortest description of a unit's requirements & function.

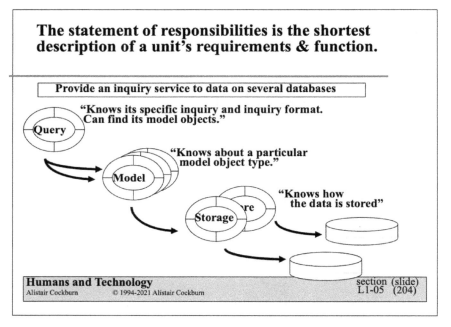

Humans and Technology
Alistair Cockburn   © 1994-2021 Alistair Cockburn

section (slide)
L1-05 (204)

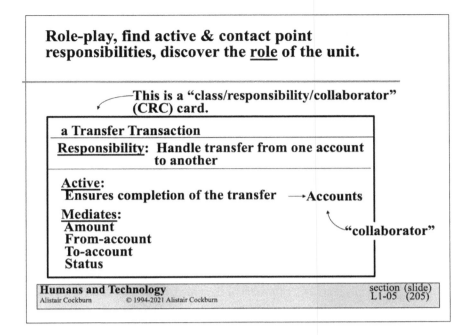

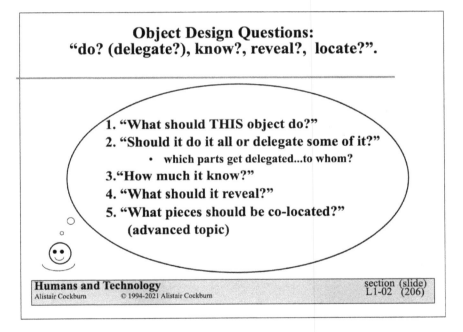

Interaction diagrams are crucial to understanding an OO design.

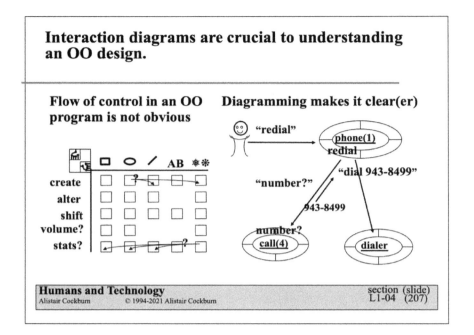

Flow of control in an OO program is not obvious

Diagramming makes it clear(er)

Typical views of an OID are top and side views; there are many ways to draw them.

Top View   **Side View**

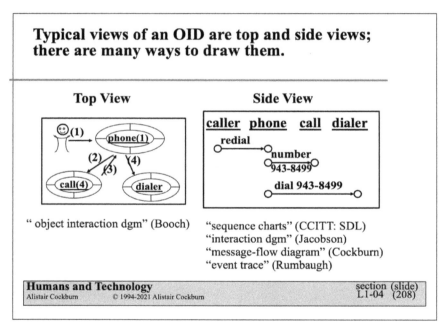

" object interaction dgm" (Booch)

"sequence charts" (CCITT: SDL)
"interaction dgm" (Jacobson)
"message-flow diagram" (Cockburn)
"event trace" (Rumbaugh)

Rule of Design: Identify classes early, but leave inheritance to language-specific class design.

1. Identify which classes are needed.
2. Identify commonality between classes.
3. Let the class designer decide how best to implement the commonality
   - Interface inheritance
   - Subclassing
   - Instance data

...A system model separating domain & application from transformers.

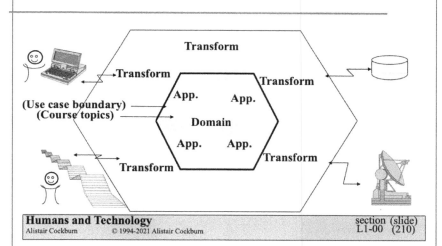

Design 2: Model and multiple interactors

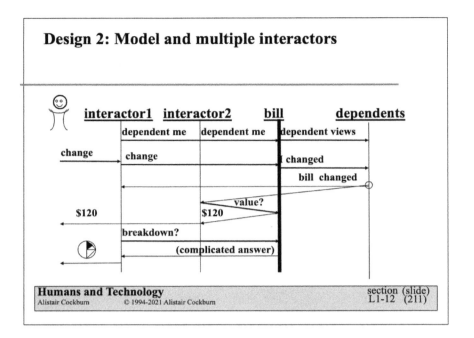

(T1) Focus on the end result: adapt to whatever is needed to deliver.

OO development is different. You will want to change many things about the way you work.

    Small, deep teams

    Increments, iterations, evolutionary prototypes.

    Matrixed ownership (class x function)

    No baseline estimation curves.

Ask not for more time, ask for more flexibility rules.

    Reduced intermediate deliverables

    Incomplete requirements

    Timeboxing

Exercises

E0. Bank (a "pre"-exercise)   Design in an "object" manner an entire bank branch office (not just the computer part) :ustomers, money, checks, places to put money, reports. Discuss how to document the design and document some part of it.

E1. Comparing Dates (messages)   Class participation: Show how two dates decide which one is greater than the other. Requires 8 people.

E2. Pizza delivery (objects)   Sketch a computerized system for recording pizza deliveries. Decide first on the menu for your pizza shop. Decide on the number of delivery zones to be handled. Take from order pickup to payment. Decide on the objects. Discuss how to document the design.

E3. Bank accounts (Inheritance)   Design one part of a banking program: different kinds of accounts. Decide what kinds of accounts your bank will support, and what variations within each. Identify the classes, possible inheritance structure, polymorphism; how to open, close, use each account.

E4a. Human coffee machine (responsibilities in partitioning)

Design a coffee machine out of humans, with humans carrying out all the operations. Decide what each person is to handle. Document the design with responsibility statements and interaction diagrams. First, design a simple coffee machine. When it works, add complexity and features. The instructor will add more variations. Watch how responsibilities are assigned and change with the changing assumptions and requirements. Introspect and discuss.

E4b. Coffee machine requirements (use cases, goals, goal failure) Create requirements for your coffee machine: actors, goals, responsibilities, goal failures. Use the 4-column functional requirements chart.

E4c. Coffee machine controller (Models and shields) Design a controller for your coffee machine. Do robustness analysis. Document the design using responsibility summaries and interaction diagrams.

E5a. Pricing requirements (Recursive Design and Incremental Development)

Write requirements for a simply price management system. Note that the price of your goods is based on component costs, plus costs that depend on other department, and that prices change over time. Identify primary, secondary actors, the service of your system. Identify the first increment of work.

E5. Pricing design   Design the first increment of the pricing system. Find the key objects and responsibilities. Assume the presence of standard system services. Document the components, responsibilities needed. Check for rpbustness. Time permitting, move on to the second increment.

E6. Sorted collections

Design a transaction log, ordering by date, initially.   Assume a component is available called a "sorted collection", which automagically keeps things sorted according to whatever function you name. Name the function it will need. Once you have an idea how to make the log, figure out how the sorted collection works. Make it work with different sorting functions, sorting any kind of object. Class participation: test your design using people.

Humans and Technology
Alistair Cockburn   © 1994-2021 Alistair Cockburn

section (slide)
L1-Ex (213)

Most of these exercises don't survive today. The coffee machine exercise is an exception. I taught it for years, and wrote about it in detail in a pair of articles for the C++ Journal. Those two articles (the preprints) are still on the archive of my old web site, at https://web.archive.org/web/20140329205954/http://alistair.cockburn.us/Coffee+machine+design+problem,+part+1 and https://web.archive.org/web/20140329205958/http://alistair.cockburn.us/Coffee+machine+design+problem,+part+2 . I recommend you really try out the exercises as they are stated in those articles and see what you think about my answers.

Also, in case you are interested in pattern-writing and design ideas, you might enjoy "A use of the endgame design strategy". I called patterns 'strategies' back then. They effectively mean the same thing, it turns out. Check it out here: https://web.archive.org/web/20140329210113/http://alistair.cockburn.us/A+use+of+the+endgame+design+strategy.

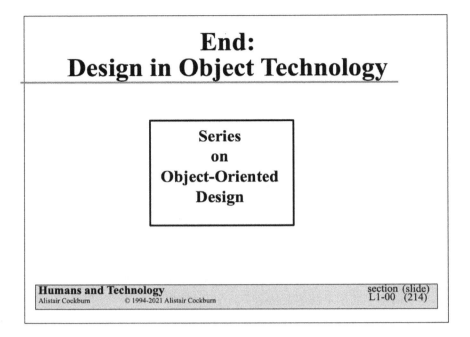

The end

Design in Object Technology
The Annotated Class of 1994
Back stories and reflections

Series on
Object-Oriented
Design

Alistair Cockburn

Lightning Source UK Ltd.
Milton Keynes UK
UKHW050930171022
410608UK00015BA/743